L.F.

Of
Human
Bondage

Coming of
Age in
the Novel

TWAYNE'S MASTERWORK STUDIES
ROBERT LECKER, GENERAL EDITOR

Of Human Bondage

Coming of Age in the Novel

ARCHIE K. LOSS

TWAYNE PUBLISHERS • BOSTON

A DIVISION OF G. K. HALL & CO.

Of Human Bondage: Coming of Age in the Novel
Archie K. Loss

Twayne's Masterwork Studies No. 40

Copyright 1990 by G. K. Hall & Co.
All rights reserved.
Published by Twayne Publishers
A division of G. K. Hall & Co.
70 Lincoln Street, Boston, Massachusetts 02111

Copyediting supervised by Barbara Sutton.
Book production by Gabrielle B. McDonald.

Typeset in 10/14 pt. Sabon
by Compositors Corporation of Cedar Rapids, Iowa 52402

Printed on permanent durable acid-free paper
and bound in the United States of America

Library of Congress Cataloging-in-Publication Data

Loss, Archie K. (Archie Krug)
    Of human bondage : coming of age in the novel / Archie K. Loss.
       p.   cm. — (Twayne's masterwork studies ; no. 40)
    Includes bibliographical references.
    Includes Index.
    ISBN 0-8057-8067-X (alk. paper). — ISBN 0-8057-8112-9 (pbk. :
  alk. paper)
    1. Maugham, W. Somerset (William Somerset), 1874–1965. Of human
bondage.   I. Title. II. Series.
PR6025.A86056   1990
823'.912—dc20   89-36944
                                            CIP

CONTENTS

A NOTE ON THE REFERENCES AND ACKNOWLEDGMENTS

The text of *Of Human Bondage* I have used throughout this book is the commonly available Penguin edition. Like most of the popular editions of this novel over the years since its initial publication, this edition has small print and rather narrow margins. It is a shame that a more readable inexpensive edition of Maugham's best book is not available, but until such an edition comes along this one will have to do. The text is at least relatively free of errors, though I have had no opportunity to review it critically.

I want to thank Norma Hartner of the secretarial staff of the Division of Humanities and Social Sciences at Penn State–Behrend College for her help with the preparation of the final manuscript of this book. I also want to thank my son Christopher, who, required to read Maugham's novel at school, has made many valuable suggestions about what should and should not be said for the benefit of the intended audience—the general reader.

W. Somerset Maugham
Courtesy of the Photography Collection, Harry Ransom Humanities Research Center, University of Texas at Austin.

CHRONOLOGY: W. SOMERSET MAUGHAM'S LIFE AND WORKS

1874   William Somerset Maugham born in Paris 25 January, the fourth
        son of Edith and Robert Ormond Maugham, a lawyer who han-
        dles the affairs of the British Embassy.

1882   Mother dies of consumption and complications of childbirth 31
        January, six days after Maugham's eighth birthday. Britain in-
        vades and conquers Egypt. Germany, Austria, and Italy form Tri-
        ple Alliance. In Berlin, Robert Koch announces the discovery of
        the bacillus causing tuberculosis.

1884   Father dies of cancer 24 June, leaving an estate of less than five
        thousand pounds for his five sons; Maugham goes to England to
        live with his Uncle Henry, vicar of the parish of All Saints in
        Whitstable, Kent, and German-born Aunt Sophie.

1885   Enters King's School in Canterbury.

1887   Queen Victoria's Golden Jubilee.

1889   Leaves King's School after recuperating from pleurisy in Hyères,
        in the south of France.

1890   Goes to Germany to attend the University of Heidelberg and
        there meets English aesthete Ellingham Brooks, with whom he
        has his first homosexual affair; is also exposed to Schopenhauer
        and other early influences.

1892   Returns to England and tries hand at accounting, which he gives
        up after one month; finally elects to study medicine at St.
        Thomas's Hospital in London, where he gains much experience
        of value to his early writing.

1894   Captain Dreyfus, in a famous case involving anti-Semitism, is
        convicted on false treason charge in France.

1895   X-rays are developed by German physicist Wilhelm Roentgen;
        Oscar Wilde goes on trial in England for sodomy.

1897	Publishes first novel, *Lisa of Lambeth*, to favorable reviews; also passes his medical exams, though has already decided against practice.
1898	Publishes second novel, *The Making of a Saint*, the first of a series of books that achieve moderate success at best; spends this year and part of the next in Spain.
1899	Completes "The Artistic Temperament of Stephen Carey," an early version of *Of Human Bondage*, but his publisher turns it down. The Boer, or South African, War begins, between the British and the Boers (descendants of Dutch settlers).
1900	The Boxer Rebellion begins in China.
1901	Death of Queen Victoria; Edward VII succeeds to the throne.
1903	*A Man of Honour*, Maugham's first play to be produced in England, opens 22 February at the Stage Society and runs for only two performances.
1904	Meets Gerald Kelly, the painter, who paints Maugham many times and becomes a lifelong friend. Britain and France form *Entente Cordiale*.
1905	Moves to Paris, where he becomes acquainted with Arnold Bennett. The Russo-Japanese War ends, with Russia victorious. General strike in Russia; *Potemkin* mutiny and reforms of the Czar. Einstein develops the theory of relativity.
1906	Travels to Greece and Egypt, the first of his longer journeys, and then returns to London to live; in April meets Ethelwyn Sylvia Jones ("Sue"), daughter of playwright Henry Arthur Jones and the model for Rosie Driffield in *Cakes and Ale;* they have an affair.
1907	*Lady Frederick* opens on the London stage 26 October, becoming Maugham's first great theatrical success.
1908	Has four plays running at the same time in the West End by midyear.
1910	As one of the most successful playwrights in the history of the British theater, takes his first trip to the United States; also meets Hugh Walpole, the original of Alroy Kear in *Cakes and Ale,* and Syrie Barnardo Wellcome, with whom he later has an affair that leads to marriage.
1912	The Balkan Wars begin over territorial disputes involving Turkey, Bulgaria, Serbia, Greece, Montenegro, and Romania.
1913	Sue Jones rejects Maugham's marriage proposal. Suffragettes demonstrate in London.
1914	Joins an ambulance unit in France as a Red Cross volunteer;

Chronology: W. Somerset Maugham's Life and Works

meets Gerald Haxton, who becomes his lifelong secretary, companion, and lover. World War I begins in August, after the assassination of Archduke Francis Ferdinand at Sarajevo in June.

1915   *Of Human Bondage* appears on both sides of the Atlantic to an initially weak reception; a sympathetic review by Theodore Dreiser in the *New Republic* brings the book the attention it deserves. Syrie gives birth to a child, Liza; Maugham is the father. Maugham meanwhile joins the British Intelligence Service, an experience that leads to the adventures recounted later in *Ashenden.*

1916   Begins writing for the theater again, with the comedy *Caroline.* Sets out on first journey to the East, from which he will derive so much material for his fiction, with Gerald Haxton as his companion. In San Francisco, on his way, meets wealthy broker Bert Alanson, who will prove important to his future fortune.

1917   Marries Syrie, who is now finally divorced, 26 May in Jersey City, New Jersey. By summer accepts offer from the Intelligence Service to undertake a mission to Russia, now in the throes of the Revolution; the trip brings on a bout of tuberculosis that puts him in a sanatorium.

1919   In April *The Moon and Sixpence* appears in England; its view of heterosexual relations reflects the deterioration of his relationship with Syrie.

1921   *The Circle,* his finest play, opens on 3 March in London; in September his most famous short story, "Rain," appears in the collection *The Trembling of a Leaf.*

1922   Mussolini comes to power in Italy.

1924   The death of Lenin and emergence of Stalin as head of Russian state.

1926   Buys a house on the French Riviera, to be called the Villa Mauresque, where he will live with Gerald Haxton; he and Syrie formalize their arrangement to live apart. General strike in Britain.

1927   Syrie decides to file for divorce, an action completed two years later.

1928   *Ashenden* appears.

1929   U.S. stock market collapses, triggering worldwide depression.

1930   *Cakes and Ale* appears to great success, partly because it is viewed as a *roman à clef;* Maugham reaches the height of his popularity as an author during this decade.

1933	His last play, *Sheppey,* opens in September in London. Hitler comes to power in Germany.
1934	Maugham renews his acquaintance with Eddie Marsh, who will be important to the editing of his manuscripts from now until Marsh's death in 1953.
1937	Leaves for India in December to gather material for *The Razor's Edge.*
1938	Publishes *The Summing Up.*
1939	The Nazis invade Poland; World War II begins.
1940–41	Leaves France with Gerald when the Nazis invade. Ultimately settles alone in a house built for him in South Carolina by his American publisher, Nelson Doubleday; travels throughout the United States giving speeches on behalf of the British war effort.
1944	Publishes *The Razor's Edge,* his last important novel. Gerald dies, leaving Maugham devastated.
1945	Alan Searle becomes Maugham's new secretary-companion.
1946	Returns with Alan to France and the Villa Mauresque, where they are to reside for Maugham's remaining years.
1948	Publishes last novel, *Catalina.*
1955	Syrie dies. In the years that follow, Maugham's relationship with his daughter Liza deteriorates, along with his mental health.
1965	Maugham dies 15 December.

1

HISTORICAL CONTEXT

As the eighteenth century was coming to a close and the Western world was trembling in the aftermath of the French Revolution, an important event took place in the history of the novel. In the years 1795–96, the great German author Johann Wolfgang von Goethe (1749–1832), best known for the poetic drama *Faust* (1808), published *Wilhelm Meisters Lehrjahre*. This novel, which describes the growth and development of a young man up to the point where he is ready to be responsible for his own life, defined the possibilities of a type of novel that was soon important in the German- and English-speaking worlds—a novel that came to be called by the German name *bildungsroman*.

The bildungsroman—literally the novel (*roman*) of development or formation of character (*bildung*)—typically begins with the childhood and early youth of a male protagonist, focusing on the obstacles, personal and societal, in the path of his development. Essentially, the bildungsroman is a novel of character, concerned primarily with the inner development of its hero. External events are important as they define or shape that inner development. The bildungsroman is less a specific kind of novel (as, say, the sonnet is a specific kind of poem) than it is a subject for a novel. Its author—often writing about himself and his own experiences—is less concerned with formal questions than with the pursuit of his particular truth. Very often, in fact, the form of the novel is dictated entirely by the events of the author's own life.[1]

If Goethe's *Wilhelm Meisters Lehrjahre* is the seed of the bildungs-roman, W. Somerset Maugham's *Of Human Bondage* (1915) is one of its later blossomings. Throughout the nineteenth century and the early part of the twentieth, the growth and development of young men was an important subject in the German and the English novel. In the English novel, Dickens provided an especially fine example of the type in *The Personal History of David Copperfield* (1850), based heavily on his own personal experiences. Other important examples include Thackeray's *The History of Pendennis* (1849–50), George Meredith's *The Ordeal of Richard Feverel* (1859), and Samuel Butler's *The Way of All Flesh* (1903). The last named, with its portrait of the troubled relationship between Ernest Pontifex and his tyrannical clergyman father, was of particular importance to Maugham.

Maugham's contemporaries were drawn to the same subject matter. In 1907 E. M. Forster's *The Longest Journey* appeared, in 1913 D. H. Lawrence's *Sons and Lovers,* and in 1916, just one year after the publication of *Of Human Bondage,* James Joyce's *A Portrait of the Artist as a Young Man.* All of these novels are examples of the bildungsroman, though each particularizes its hero's development with events from the author's own life. Most celebrated of all in its day, though now viewed as less significant than any of the novels mentioned, was Compton Mackenzie's *Sinister Street* (1913–14). Mackenzie's approach to the novel—which is heavily chronological, achieving credibility through accretion of detail—is very similar to Maugham's way of telling the story of Philip Carey.

In the end, however, all novels of the bildungsroman type have many similarities, no matter how different the lives of their authors. It is difficult to imagine two authors more different than Maugham and Joyce, yet when they choose to write about their own experiences in growing up, the results conform to an extraordinary extent to the norms of the bildungsroman.

Both novelists present the reader with heroes tormented by their sexuality. Though their circumstances differ in details, both Philip Carey, Maugham's hero, and Stephen Dedalus, Joyce's, have great difficulty accepting and defining for themselves this most fundamental aspect of their humanity. Both Philip and Stephen also rebel against the values of their homes and their religions. In addition, they both find exile from their native countries necessary to their personal development: Philip spends time in both Germany and France in his search for himself, and Stephen leaves Ireland at the end of Joyce's novel, on his way to France. Both Philip and Stephen are afflicted with physical disabilities: Stephen has poor eyesight, Philip a clubfoot. Stephen wants to be an artist in words, Philip in paint. Finally, both Philip's and Stephen's stories, different as they are in form and style, end on what is essentially an optimistic note. How else, in telling of his beginnings, can an artist end his tale?

This is not to suggest, however, that Maugham or Joyce or Lawrence or Forster or Mackenzie or any other author of bildungsromans followed some kind of formula—not deliberately, at least. What such authors did was more or less what Maugham did: finding the details of their own lives pressing so forcibly upon them, they put aside everything else to put their experiences down on paper. It is a way of clearing the air—or, more precisely, the mind—of the residue of the years. Each of these authors had to feel that he was telling the story for the first time, just as each of us must feel, to some extent at least, that we are the first person to experience the events of our lives.

Of Human Bondage, both in subject matter and in technique, represents a significant departure from everything Maugham had written previously. It is heavily autobiographical, dealing with facts and people from Maugham's own experience. It is also extremely long and detailed—the longest of Maugham's novels. Unlike his well-known comedies, it presents a painful picture of life—part of the dark underside of the late Victorian England in which Maugham grew into manhood. The comedies and early novels had established Maugham as a popular author; *Of Human Bondage*—though not overwhelmingly successful at the time of publication—made him important.

It appeared as England was coming to the realization that World War I would last longer than anyone had expected. The initial reviews were not outstanding, perhaps because one more book about the development of one more young man seemed somewhat irrelevant when more and more young men were losing their lives in France. The novel was destined, however, to become a modern classic.

2

THE IMPORTANCE OF
THE WORK

> . . . I was no sooner firmly established as the most popular dramatist of
> the day than I began once more to be obsessed by the teeming memo-
> ries of my past life. They came back to me so pressingly, in my sleep, on
> my walks, at rehearsals, at parties, they became such a burden to me,
> that I made up my mind there was only one way to be free of them and
> that was to write them all down on paper. (6)

Thus Maugham writes of the inception of *Of Human Bondage* in his
foreword to the novel written some years after its first publication. Important as the novel was to him at the time, and important as it may have
seemed to the literate public of his generation, it is a fair question why it
should still be regarded as important.

Philip Carey is not a hero with whom it is easy to identify; he is not,
in a sense, a hero at all. He lacks a sense of humor, and his long, torturous
love affair with Mildred Rogers is extremely painful to read about. Whatever decisiveness he ultimately shows about his career, with Mildred he
is—at least until the very end of the book—completely at the mercy of a
nasty, indifferent person whose outlook on life is totally selfish. Philip allows Mildred to use him and then, when she needs him again, to use him

some more. It is truly a case of bondage—one human being enslaved to another—and Philip clearly enjoys being enslaved.

But there is another side to Maugham's story of Philip. This is the story of the young man who slowly gains an awareness of himself, who realizes first that he has an unnatural desire to be hurt and then finally acts on that realization and separates himself permanently from the source of his pain. In this version of events, Philip learns about himself through his suffering with Mildred and emerges as a fuller, more sympathetic human being, capable of making decisions of the heart as well as the head. These are not necessarily heroic decisions, but they do reflect the application of human intelligence to the ordinary affairs of life, and to this extent the reader can readily identify with them. If Philip is not a conventional hero, he is at least a character who, like many of us, learns from experience.

In addition to being of personal value to the reader, *Of Human Bondage* also has historical importance for its record of life in the 1890s and turn-of-the-century England, Germany, and France. It does not deal with great events, but it does provide a valuable record of life in a provincial English community, the education of a middle-class boy at a fairly typical boarding school, and the training of a medical student at this time in England. In these portions of the novel, as well as those set in Heidelberg and Paris, Maugham writes directly from his own experience.

From the historical standpoint, *Of Human Bondage* is important in another respect. It provides a short, popular summary of many major trends in the philosophical thinking of the period. Beginning with his stay at Heidelberg early in the novel and ending with his relationship with Thorpe Athelny toward the end, Philip (like Maugham) has an interest in philosophical ideas. Through this interest, the reader is exposed to the thought of Spinoza, Schopenhauer, Kant, and other major figures in the history of ideas, as well as to concepts not readily associated with particular philosophers, such as aestheticism and hedonism.

Of Human Bondage does not make a contribution in any sense to the formal history of the novel. Its importance lies rather in what it says about its subject—a young man coming of age. Here, Maugham's words from the foreword are significant: "I no longer sought a jewelled prose and a rich texture on unavailing attempts to achieve which I had formerly wasted much labour; I sought on the contrary plainness and simplicity. With so much that I wanted to say within reasonable limits I felt that I could not afford to waste words and I set out now with the notion of using only such as were necessary to make my meaning clear" (6).

The same might be said of the form the novel takes: only as many scenes (some readers think there are too many) occur as Maugham thought necessary to make the meaning of Philip's life clear. If the rigidly chronological approach Maugham takes becomes somewhat predictable, it does create a narrative of great solidity. At least until the final chapters of the book, when Philip falls in love with one of Athelny's daughters, the story is almost too painfully credible—a fine example of narrative fiction in the realistic tradition.

3

CRITICAL RECEPTION

In 1897, as a medical student in his last year of study, Maugham published his first novel, *Liza of Lambeth,* a tale of the London streets. Based on personal observation of London's poor during his internship, the novel brought Maugham recognition and encouraged him to make writing, not medicine, his profession. Between the publication of *Liza of Lambeth* and the publication of *Of Human Bondage* in 1915, he wrote seven other novels, none of which is remembered today, and established himself as the foremost writer of drawing-room comedy for the English stage.

Maugham's approach to the writing of novels was much like his approach to writing for the stage: he was essentially a commercial writer, interested in earning a living by his work and willing to try writing different kinds of novels to develop a readership. In the same sense, he learned to write comedy for the stage because it was popular and would guarantee him an income that more serious work would not produce.

Each of his eight early novels differs somewhat from the others, and each helped Maugham to develop a different aspect of his writing talent. Novelists in those days were expected to write a novel almost every year, and the reading public looked forward to the event much as the movie-going public now looks forward to the new efforts of its favorite directors. These novels did not establish Maugham as a major writer, but they proved him to be a capable one. He was clearly a developing craftsman, someone to be contended with. In none of the early novels, however, did he have the opportunity to speak from his own experience, in his own voice. When that opportunity came, the book that resulted surprised the reading public and made it reconsider its attitude toward Maugham as a writer of fiction.

Of Human Bondage is extremely long, in part very unpleasant in its subject matter, and written in a style unlike that of Maugham's earlier novels. In those novels Maugham aspired to language not entirely natural to him—a reflection of the tendency of the day toward inflated vocabulary and what is often termed hothouse prose. In telling the story of Philip Carey, Maugham relied on relatively simple, straightforward language and on a style that is extremely literal. Small wonder that certain critics and general readers as well had trouble accepting what he had done.

A further problem in the initial reception of the book was that it followed a series of books about the development of young men (the bildungsromans referred to earlier) and inevitably seemed to imitate them. Throughout his career as a writer, Maugham suffered from criticism that his work was imitative, unoriginal; the same criticism to some extent plagued the reception of his finest novel.

The book was not ignored, however. No work by a writer of Maugham's already quite substantial reputation would be passed by. It was simply not appreciated for what it is—a major achievement in twentieth-century English fiction. Reviewers saw it related to one school or another, from French realism to Pre-Raphaelite, and considered it overly long, undramatic, prolix, generally weak in form. Some appreciated the intensity of certain scenes and the truthfulness of Maugham's depictions of Philip's and other characters' emotions, but the general tone of the reviews varied from condescension to disapproval. There was little enthusiasm for the novel, and little encouragement to its author to do more of the same.[2]

This, at least, was the case in England. In the United States, in one of those instances of a major novelist reviewing the work of one soon to be regarded as such, Maugham's novel received something closer to its just deserts. The reviewer was the great American realist, Theodore Dreiser (1871–1945), author of *Sister Carrie* (1900) and *An American Tragedy* (1925). The review appeared in the *New Republic* of 25 December 1915, and began with a paean to the novel that must have been better than any Christmas gift Maugham received that year: "Sometimes in retrospect of a great book the mind falters, confused by the multitude and yet the harmony of the detail, the strangeness of the frettings, the brooding, musing, intelligence that has foreseen, loved, created, elaborated, perfected, until, in this middle ground, which we call life, somewhere between nothing and nothing, hangs the perfect thing which we love and cannot understand, but which we are compelled to confess a work of art."[3]

Dreiser lists other recent novels that come to mind in reading Maugham's, including *Sinister Street,* and then gives a short summary of the story. What is most interesting in the review, however, is Dreiser's evaluation of the achievement. He sees the novel as "unmoral" and rising "to no spired climax," but, unlike most other reviewers, he does not view these qualities as defects. Rather, the novel as Maugham has written it has the qualities of the Persian rug mentioned by the poet Cronshaw, a complicated woven pattern in which each reader must find his or her own significance. Dreiser's only reservation is about the ending of the novel; there, Maugham seems to treat Philip's relationship with Sally Athelny with a "peculiar reticence." Still, Dreiser's review established beyond question the importance of *Of Human Bondage* as a novel and of Maugham as a writer. It also contributed to establishing Maugham's popularity in the United States.

The history of critical opinion is to some extent cyclic; books valued highly in their day often suffer later on, and those not valued sufficiently often achieve renown after their authors' deaths. In the case of *Of Human Bondage,* Dreiser's review signaled that it was a major achievement, and within ten years it had achieved the status of a modern classic. The dust jacket of the American edition proclaimed it as "the greatest novel of our time"; it was assigned in the classroom and compared with other major modern novels. Perhaps a reaction was inevitable.

Critical Reception

After writing a series of highly popular plays and novels that became worldwide bestsellers, Maugham had yet to achieve the first rank of world authors. The biographer Lytton Strachey put him ironically in "Class Two, Division One"; the American critic Edmund Wilson would have ranked him even lower. In 1946, he attacked the author's general reputation. "It has happened to me from time to time to run into some person of taste," he begins, "who tells me that I ought to take Somerset Maugham seriously, yet I have never been able to convince myself that he was anything but second-rate."[4] His conclusion is even more trenchant: Maugham "is for our day what Bulwer–Lytton was for Dickens's: a half-trashy novelist, who writes badly, but is patronized by half-serious readers, who do not care much about writing."[5]

By the time Wilson was writing, more than thirty years after the publication of *Of Human Bondage*, Maugham had yet to equal it in his longer fiction. He had also produced essays and volumes of memoirs that were unfavorable to certain contemporaries and showed little sympathy for modern literature, for which Wilson was a powerful spokesman. Even so, to some extent at least, the criticism hit home. Much that Maugham had written was not to be taken seriously; much was clearly written for no more inspired purpose than to make money.

All the same, four years later, in 1950, when anthologist Whit Burnett conducted a survey for a collection of representative writings by major living authors, Maugham came out high on the list.[6] Burnett's list was derived from a survey of authors, editors, journalists, critics, reviewers, educators, librarians, miscellaneous public figures, bookstore personnel, and general readers. Maugham figured most prominently in the lists from authors, editors, reviewers, United States PEN Club members, bookstore personnel, and miscellaneous public figures. Over all, he was twelfth in a list of the fifty most voted upon, with 427 votes from all sources. By comparison, Shaw, who came first on the list (and whose reputation had slipped somewhat by this time), had 539 votes. Only one other English author, Aldous Huxley, had more votes than Maugham, coming in ninth place with 434 votes. (T. S. Eliot, also counted as English by Burnett, was eighth, with 435 votes.) While a single survey, done with a selective population for one anthology, proves little about ultimate

11

worth, the people surveyed do make an impressive and certainly representative list, and the results are fairly indicative of Maugham's general standing in the literary world of 1950, toward the end of his long career.

Certainly Maugham's reputation has diminished since 1950. Most of his work is in print in one form or another, but beyond the short stories and a few novels and plays, probably not much of it is read. This suggests that those who argued, like Wilson, that Maugham was second-rate were right. But no one, however anxious to see Maugham's work relegated to the second rank or below, will deny that *Of Human Bondage* is a significant achievement in fiction.

A READING

4

MAJOR THEMES:
BONDAGE AND TROUBLED GRACE

Implicit in the concept of the bildungsroman is the idea of growth. It is not enough that the main character should simply experience a succession of adventures or suffer from the pangs of unrequited love; he must grow in understanding and sense of responsibility as a result of his adventures or loves. In the broadest sense, that is what the bildungsroman is about: following the main character to the point at which he is ready to assume responsibility for his life.

Of Human Bondage follows this pattern. It begins with the death of Philip's mother when he is a boy of ten and ends with Philip in his late twenties, his medical training complete, ready to assume adult responsibilities, his bride-to-be by his side. Thematically, it shows the growth of Philip's sense of reality, of his ability to distinguish what is true from what is false in the world around him and in his innermost being. It is only when Philip is able to reconcile to some extent the contradictions he perceives in himself and in the world that the novel achieves its end. To reach that goal, Maugham develops two major themes.

The first of these centers on the idea of bondage. Philip's relationship with Mildred is the primary vehicle for the development of this theme. Philip's bondage to Mildred is both physical and emotional—

physical in the sense that he needs to have her by his side or be with her even if she doesn't want him around, emotional in the sense that whether he is with her or not she dominates his thoughts and actions as if she were actually there. From the beginning of their relationship, when Philip finds he cannot keep himself from going back to the tearoom where she works as a waitress, till the penultimate episode in their career, when Mildred, having had an affair with Griffiths, leaves Philip with the hated epithet "cripple," his feelings are the same.

Even after Philip realizes (fairly early in the relationship) that his attraction to Mildred is sick, he is still bound to her. Philip never has sexual relations with Mildred, yet he wants to assume the role of provider to her and father to her baby. In the terms of psychopathology, Philip is both a masochist and a voyeur. As a masochist, he needs to suffer to justify a love relationship. As a voyeur, he enjoys creating an opportunity for Mildred to have pleasure with another man. Even the love of a woman who genuinely cares for him—Norah Nesbitt—is not enough to change the pattern of his behavior. Before that can change, he has to hit bottom emotionally and economically.

The bondage theme also appears in relationship to other characters. Philip's Aunt Louisa lives in bondage to his Uncle William, the Vicar of Whitstable. Catering to his every whim, denying herself things she needs, Louisa is almost a parody of the wife as doormat so common to Victorian fiction. Hayward, Philip's friend from Heidelberg days, lives in bondage to a false ideal: an aesthetic view of life that prevents him from acting. He is the eternal dilettante, fluttering like a butterfly from flower to flower. Fanny Price, whose devotion to art is so misplaced and whose failure provides such a lesson to Philip in his Paris years, lives in bondage to an ideal she can never realize. Foinet's advice, savage as it is, is right: she is no artist, and chooses suicide over admitting the truth of his judgment. Cronshaw, another Paris friend who greatly influences Philip's view of the world, is in bondage to alcohol and a way of life that will ultimately destroy him. Cronshaw shows the dark side of the Bohemian life that appealed to Philip so much in his reading. These characters and others illustrate the pervasiveness of the bondage theme.

At the same time Philip puts himself into a state of bondage, however, he seeks independence. At King's School, he will not agree to try for an Oxford scholarship despite his admiration for the headmaster, Perkins, because he does not want to be ordained. Time and time again, in decisions about his studies and career, he asserts his independence from his uncle, who despairs of exerting any influence over him. Philip ultimately chooses medicine as his profession, much as he had tried art, because he believes it will give him the freedom he needs to survive. At the end of the novel, on the other hand, he almost decides against marriage because he is afraid it will limit his horizons and keep him from doing what he wants.

In describing Philip's ruminations on the subjects of marriage and personal freedom, Maugham makes use of the phrase "a more troubling grace." It occurs late in the novel, in chapter CVI, after Mildred has left Philip for the last time and he has come under the hedonistic influence of Thorpe Athelny. Running through the novel as a metaphor of Philip's frequent confusion of purpose is the image of a Persian carpet, first suggested to him in Paris by Cronshaw. In such a carpet, Cronshaw suggests, one might find the meaning of life. Philip, pondering his fate, thinks of that carpet again:

> In the vast warp of life . . . , with the background to his fancies that there was no meaning and that nothing was important, a man might get a personal satisfaction in selecting the various strands that worked out the pattern. There was one pattern, the most obvious, perfect, and beautiful, in which a man was born, grew to manhood, married, produced children, toiled for his bread, and died; but there were others, intricate and wonderful, in which happiness did not enter and in which success was not attempted; and in them might be discovered a more troubling grace. (524–25)

The "more troubling grace" of Philip's thoughts suggests at least a halfway point between the bondage of his relationship to Mildred and the ideal of a relationship, like the Athelnys', in which a lifetime is spent with a single partner. Like that ideal, Philip's more troubled grace is also an alternative of sorts to the absolute meaninglessness of life to which he has by now assented, after the death of Cronshaw and his friend

Hayward ("There was no meaning in life, and man by living served no end. It was immaterial whether he was born or not born, whether he lived or ceased to live. Life was insignificant and death without consequence" [524].) Instead of the bleak prospect of a life totally without meaning, Philip can envision at least some figure in the carpet, "intricate and wonderful, in which happiness did not enter and success was not attempted."

Given these thoughts of Philip's, is it reasonable for him to choose the pattern that is "the most obvious, perfect, and beautiful, in which a man . . . married, produced children, toiled for his bread, and died," especially since he has made other plans and Sally is in fact not pregnant? In other words, is the ending of the novel honest? Or is Maugham pandering to his reading audience, giving it what he thinks it wants rather than what, logically, it should have? Every reader has to make his or her own decision on this matter.

Inevitably, in reaching that decision, the reader will be influenced by what he or she knows about Maugham's own attitudes toward marriage, love, and life. *Of Human Bondage* is an autobiographical novel: "fact and fiction are inextricably mingled," Maugham wrote in his foreword; "the emotions are my own, but not all of the incidents are related as they happened, and some of them are transferred to my hero not from my own life but from that of persons with whom I was intimate" (7). But to what extent does Philip Carey constitute Maugham's *alter ego?*

In terms of his physical characteristics and psychology, Philip is remarkably similar to his creator, though some details may have been altered. To cite only one example, Maugham suffered from a stammer that made ordinary spoken communication extremely difficult for him, especially when he was a child. In Philip's character, that difficulty is transformed into a clubfoot that makes him self-conscious and the butt of jokes at school.

Other matters can be addressed more readily now that a definitive biography of Maugham has appeared, with Ted Morgan's *Maugham* (1980).[7] Morgan had access to materials that Maugham did not wish his executors to make available to anyone, and he also had the advantage of researching and writing his biography at a time when many of

Maugham's friends and colleagues were still alive. His book illuminates many characters and scenes from *Of Human Bondage* and helps to shed light on some of the novel's more ambiguous passages. It also helps the reader to establish the chronology of events in the novel as compared with those of Maugham's life.[8]

One aspect of Maugham confirmed by Morgan's biography enters into Philip's character in subtle ways. Throughout most of his early adult life, Maugham was bisexual, attracted, often simultaneously, to men and to women. As he approached his marriage with Sylvie Barnardo, for instance, he began an affair with Gerald Haxton that was to outlast the marriage and contribute to its demise. In the novel, Philip shows no overt homosexual behavior, though at times he obviously feels considerable attraction to men. This attraction constitutes a kind of subtheme of the novel and may account in part for the dissatisfaction one feels at its ending.

For many characters other than Philip, it is apparent that Maugham drew directly from his own experience. Uncle William and Aunt Louisa, for example, are precise portraits of Maugham's real-life uncle and aunt. Equally precise, apparently, is the portrait of Etheridge Hayward, based on Ellingham Brooks, whom Maugham actually met in Heidelberg. For other characters, however, there is no key. Most notable among these, the model for Mildred remains unknown. One can imagine that in creating characters as in describing events Maugham employed the freedom he suggests in his foreword, in some cases perhaps for reasons that had nothing to do with aesthetics.

In terms of chronology, the novel follows Maugham's early life fairly closely, though certain events are transposed or omitted, creating gaps of several years. In the novel, Philip's father is already dead by the time his mother dies; Philip becomes an orphan on his way to the vicarage at Whitstable within a few pages of the opening of the book. In real life, Maugham's father outlived his mother by several years. Maugham's mother died in 1882 (in Paris, not London), his father in 1884; in the novel, Philip's mother dies in 1885.

Another difference occurs later in the novel, when Philip decides to study art in Paris. Although artists were to occupy Maugham's attention in more than one story, he was never an art student and did not live in Paris during the corresponding period of his life. At the time Philip is in Paris, the young Maugham was already a medical student in London. Maugham did spend a year-and-a-half in Heidelberg, but, on the other hand, only one month studying accounting as compared with Philip's year.

As interesting as such connections are, however, *Of Human Bondage* must ultimately be judged on its own merits as a novel; works of art are independent of the lives of their creators, no matter how closely they are allied. In the pages that follow, we will read the novel as a work of fiction with the major themes of bondage and troubled grace. If to some extent this reading repeats the events of the story, it should be kept in mind that any treatment of a novel so heavily chronological, built out of a series of incidents in the life of its main character, must itself be chronological and summary. Let us hope, however, that out of such a review will emerge the generalizations important to a critical judgment of the novel. Let us hope, too, that this reading will improve the enjoyment of the novel for a generation of readers now more than eight decades removed from the characters and events it describes.

5

DISORDER AND EARLY SORROW: PHILIP'S CHILDHOOD AND YOUTH

Modern psychology has taught us that the early years of childhood are important in the formation of character; from the time of our first perceptions until we enter school, we have many of our most significant experiences. This truth, now part of common knowledge, has been familiar to poets and novelists for centuries. It certainly informs the opening chapters of *Of Human Bondage*, lending them a poignancy that influences our judgments of Philip Carey ever after in the book.

The key elements in Philip's childhood are those over which he has no control: the death of his parents, orphaning him at the age of ten; his lack of money; a home life with a childless uncle and aunt; and, most important of all, a physical disability that plagues him throughout his life. All of these circumstances dictate, one way or another, what happens to Philip as he develops into a young adult. All of them decisively influence his behavior both as a child and as a young man.

Of the two parents he loses, his mother is the one who means more to him. His father, a surgeon who dies of blood poisoning, is a shadowy figure whose influence emerges, albeit indirectly, later on. Next to his nurse, Emma, Philip's mother is the person to whom he is closest as a child. Her death from childbirth, only six months after his father dies, is an indelible loss. For him, time stops when his mother dies. Given the opportunity to take something in memory of her, Philip chooses "a little clock that he had once heard his mother say she liked" (15).

A beautiful but impractical woman, Mrs. Carey did not manage well the resources left by her husband. After her death, only two thousand pounds remain: not much to raise and educate properly a young boy in the late nineteenth century. The need for money becomes a major theme in the story from these opening chapters on. At this point it is Reverend Carey who understands its importance best. He can't help gloating over the fact that his dead brother, who seemed to live so much better than he, should leave his only child in such a plight: "the Vicar felt the satisfaction of the prophet who saw fire and brimstone consume the city which would not mend its way to his warning" (20). When, later in the novel, Monsieur Foinet advises Philip, "Money is like a sixth sense without which you cannot make a complete use of the other five" (248), his words have unusual weight because of Philip's experiences with an inadequate income. At the end of the novel, ironically enough, it is Philip's modest inheritance from his uncle that allows him to return to medical school and complete his studies after he loses his money through some bad investments.

Of more significance to the young Philip than lack of money, however, is the physical disability he must endure. His dying mother sobs when she passes her hand over his left foot, in recognition of its imperfection, but Philip sobs more throughout his childhood when, time after time, he is reminded that he is physically different from other boys. This difference contributes to his self-consciousness and aloofness; this in turn leads to a neurotic possessiveness of the few friends he manages to make. From the early chapters in Blackstable, when Philip prays to wake up with his disability gone, to virtually the last, Philip's feelings about his disability are important to the novel. They especially help to explain why he allows himself to become so attached to Mildred when it is apparent from the beginning that she doesn't care about him. He seems to want her approval in spite of his foot and from early in their relationship calls attention to it. Only toward the end of the novel, after he has an operation to correct the worst of his defect, does its effect on his life diminish.

By then it seems so much less important than other things that he is finally able to put it into perspective.

Philip's disability has a symbolic significance typical of the bildungsroman, in which the main character usually suffers from some physical defect that makes his growth and development difficult. Rickie Elliot, the protagonist of E. M. Forster's *The Longest Journey,* is also lame; Stephen Dedalus, of James Joyce's *A Portrait of the Artist as a Young Man,* suffers from the weak eyesight of his creator. In other novels of this kind, the defect of the hero may be internal or wholly imagined, the sense of difference psychological rather than real. In D. H. Lawrence's *Sons and Lovers,* Paul Morel's mother looks at him as an infant and has these thoughts: "Her heart was heavy because of the child, almost as if it were unhealthy, or malformed. Yet it seemed quite well. But she noticed the peculiar knitting of the baby's brows, and the peculiar heaviness of its eyes, as if it were trying to understand something that was pain."[9] For all heroes of the bildungsroman, learning about life is essentially a painful experience.

Living with a childless uncle and aunt does not make Philip's experience easier. Life at Blackstable, on the Kentish coast, revolves entirely around the vicar and his duties. Much later in the novel, after his uncle's death, Philip comes across a letter from his mother to his uncle asking if he would be willing to serve as Philip's godfather. This relationship explains in part why he and his wife Louisa are willing to take on the responsibility of raising the boy when his mother dies, but in fact there is nowhere else for him to go. If his uncle looks on Philip as an inconvenience, his Aunt Louisa comes to care for the boy almost as if he were her own. Philip's childhood at Blackstable may be lonely in some respects, but it is not without love.

As the chief representative of the Church of England in a small community, Uncle William has social position but not much income. He and his wife live comfortably, but far from grandly, and their living depends upon the largesse of the wealthiest parishioners. In religion as in other areas of life, England in the late nineteenth century was class-conscious to an extent difficult to imagine today. The Anglican church was divided into two major congregations—the high, or established, church, of which Philip's uncle is a priest, and the low, or dissenting, church, also known as chapel, which had a more evangelical emphasis. Generally speaking, the low church worshippers came from the lower-middle or working classes and the high church worshippers from the upper-middle class, the gentry, and the nobility. High church worshippers considered themselves members of the true church and looked down their noses at those who attended chapel.

Even the topography of the village, as Maugham describes it early in the novel, supports this social distinction. "Blackstable was a fishing village," he writes. "It consisted of a high street in which were the shops, the bank, the doctor's house, and the houses of two or three coalship owners; round the little harbor were shabby streets in which lived fishermen and poor people; but since they went to chapel they were of no account" (23).

The Careys, as the first family of the established church, are tied to their parishioners even in their choice of shops to patronize: "Shopping in Blackstable was not a simple matter. For dissent, helped by the fact that the parish church was two miles from town, was very common; and it was necessary to deal only with churchgoers; Mrs. Carey knew perfectly that the vicarage custom might make all the difference to a trades-man's faith" (23).

Fifteen years after the publication of *Of Human Bondage,* in the novel *Cakes and Ale,* Maugham's narrator describes growing up under circumstances similar to Philip's. He writes: "Blackstable was peculiar in this that though it was on the sea, with a long shingly beach and marsh-land at the back, you had only to go about half a mile inland to come into the most rural country in Kent. Winding roads that ran between the great fat green fields and clumps of huge elms, substantial and with a homely stateliness like good old Kentish farmers' wives, high-coloured and robust, who had grown portly on good butter and home-made bread and cream and fresh eggs."[10] The tone is nostalgic, and even though the narrator admits to a snobbishness, shared by Philip, that limits his view of behavior to what is proper and what is not, there is a glow to the writing about Blackstable that is notably missing from *Of Human Bondage.* (The only chapters in *Of Human Bondage* to have this quality are also set in

Kent, however, and describe the Athelnys' hop-picking in the country-side. The same tone also asserts itself in some of the Paris chapters.)

In *Of Human Bondage,* Blackstable is notable chiefly for the limitations it imposes on Philip and his foster parents. It is a narrow existence, and it forces Philip, an only child, even further into himself. With no real friends except his uncle and aunt and their servant Mary Ann, Philip avails himself of his uncle's excellent library and develops the habit of reading: "Insensibly he formed the most delightful habit in the world, the habit of reading: he did not know that thus he was providing himself with a refuge from all the distress of life; he did not know either that he was creating for himself an unreal world which would make the real world of every day a source of bitter disappointment" (37).

Here, for the first time in the novel, occurs the important theme of the real and the ideal. Throughout most of *Of Human Bondage,* Philip tries to distinguish one from the other; he deals with the problem both philosophically and empirically, reaching a conclusion intellectually before he is able to accept it emotionally. It is possible to say, in fact, that the difference between ideal and real is at the core of Philip's relationship with Mildred, which dominates the central chapters of the book. Philip gradually comes to see the real nature of Mildred and his love for her, and as he does he becomes fuller, more human, as a person. The same distinction is also certainly at the core of much of Philip's childhood experience.

Schooling for a boy of Philip's class meant public school, and public school meant, in the nomenclature of the United States, boarding school. At about the age of ten, education for the well-to-do passed from the hands of governesses or private tutors to the halls of the public schools, where students passed from form to form (the equivalent of grades) and where instruction was the task of masters responsible for each form. Public schools were entirely masculine, both in faculty and student body, and students and faculty lived in. (There were day schools, as there were certain day students at the public schools, but both were generally considered inferior.) The great public schools of England—schools like Eton, Harrow, or Rugby—were upper-class institutions, intended to perpetuate the existing social structure by educating the heirs apparent of the best families in the values appropriate to their class. Celebrated and sentimentalized in novels like Thomas Hughes's *Tom Brown's School Days* (1857) (about Rugby) and James Hilton's *Goodbye, Mr. Chips* (1934), these schools today have somewhat less impact on the future leadership of England, but they still stand for traditional values.

Philip Carey does not attend Eton, Harrow, or Rugby, and his experience of public school comes closer to that described in George Orwell's classic essay "Such, Such Were the Joys . . ." than it does to the idealized view in the novels by Hilton or Hughes. First of all, because he is not sufficiently well-to-do, Philip is not able to go to one of the best-known schools. King's School, in Tercanbury, where he is enrolled by his uncle at the age of ten, is connected to the cathedral: "Boys were encouraged there to aspire to Holy Orders, and the education was such as might prepare an honest lad to spend his life in God's service" (38). This relatively modest aspiration suits a boy of Philip's income and class, and he becomes a student in the preparatory school attached to King's. (The preparatory schools provide several years of instruction to ready boys for the curriculum of the public school to which they are attached.) There, unused to the company of other boys and naturally shy, Philip is immediately singled out because of his deformity. He soon becomes the butt of jokes, especially because he cannot compete at games.

Orwell, who was also a student at a prep school, recounts in "Such, Such Were the Joys . . ." the importance attached to games, especially, in his case, to football: "What counted was football, at which I was funk. I loathed the game, and since I could see no pleasure or usefulness in it, it was very difficult for me to show courage at it. Football, it seemed to me, is . . . a species of fighting. The lovers of football are large, boisterous, nobbly boys who are good at knocking down and trampling on slightly smaller boys. That was the pattern of school life—a continuous triumph of the strong over the weak."[11]

The general truth that Orwell soon saw was that, like Philip, he did not fit in: "All the different kinds of virtue seemed to be mysteriously interconnected and to belong to much the same people. It was not only money that mattered: there were also strength, beauty, charm, athleticism and something called 'guts' or 'character,' which in reality meant the power to impose your will on others." This lesson Philip quickly learns.

Philip is unable to join in the games, and even when he tries to be one of the boys by playing the forbidden game of Nibs (a game for two players using the steel pens that were then standard items in school) he ends up being treated differently. His opponent, a boy named Singer, is caned for playing the game, but Philip is let off because he is a "cripple." For the rest of the term and later, Singer torments Philip whenever he has a chance.

By the time he is twelve and has reached the first form, the pattern of Philip's school life has been set. He is gifted at his studies, winning a number of prizes, and as a result is pretty much left alone. With the onset of puberty, however, he also becomes acutely self-conscious and more alienated than ever from his classmates. Maugham's general comments about Philip's feelings at this point largely describe his character throughout the novel:

> It is only by degrees, through pain, that he [the newborn child] understands the fact of the body. And experiences of the same kind are necessary for the individual to become conscious of himself; but here there is a difference that, although everyone becomes equally conscious of his body as a separate and complete organism, everyone does not become equally conscious of himself as a complete and separate personality. The feeling of apartness from others comes to most with puberty, but it is not always developed to such a degree as to make the difference between the individual and his fellows noticeable to the individual. (49)

The emphasis on the painfulness of experience especially suits Philip's character and supports one of the major themes of the novel.

But Philip's entire experience of school is not painful. He does succeed academically, at least before his last year or so, and he does make some friends. His problem with friendship is not that it is impossible for him to have friends but rather that he expects too much of the friends he has. Like many only children, he expects complete devotion from his friends. He envies boys who are physically normal, sometimes imagining himself in their place. A boy named Rose is a particular favorite, and when Rose finally rejects him because he is too demanding, Philip is distraught. This relationship has homoerotic overtones, which will be dealt with in chapter 7. For now it is enough to say that romances were not uncommon in schools where boys lived together and where companionship was entirely masculine. Such relationships were more likely to remain latent, however, like Philip's with Rose.

At the same time that Philip learns the painful lessons of life at school, he also learns to assert his independence. From very early in the novel Philip shows himself capable of self-assertion, a quality to prove increasingly important later on. However impractical or idealistic he may seem at times, his sense of reality and his independence of will ultimately assert themselves.

Shortly after he moves in with his uncle and aunt, Philip wins a small triumph that heralds things to come. The vicar is accustomed to napping every Sunday afternoon, and the household is expected to maintain complete silence. One afternoon Philip is playing with blocks and makes a noise that disturbs his uncle, who tells him that it is very wicked to play on Sunday. To make matters even worse, Philip refuses to say that he is sorry: "He did not know what power it was in him that prevented him from making any expression of regret. He felt his ears tingling, he was a little inclined to cry, but no word would issue from his lips" (32). Pressed to apologize by his aunt, Philip ends by asking to be left alone and saying that he hates her and wishes her dead (33). While her tears make him say he is sorry, he apologizes to her, not to his uncle, and he has effectively demonstrated, small and crippled though he may be, that he is not easily intimidated.

The same strength of will shows itself at Tercanbury when he is tormented by Singer. Although Philip is the smaller and weaker of the two, he tries to defend himself when Singer twists his arm or tortures him. What really bothers him is that he is forced to say he is sorry for something he has not done: "It was that which rankled with Philip: he could not bear the humiliation of apologies, which were wrung from him by pain greater than he could bear" (48).

Philip's most important assertion of will as a child—in preparation for the philosophy he attempts to develop for himself when he is older—is his decision that religion means little to him. Living in the vicarage has not improved his attitude; what determines Philip's decision, however, is his experience with praying to have his foot healed.

As he passes through a period of special devoutness—wanting to be religious because of various guilt feelings—he decides to wish for an end to his disability. The idea is simple: if I am devout, I shall be rewarded. The message of the Biblical text (Matthew 21: 21) seems plain: "And all this, whatsoever ye shall ask in prayer, believing, ye shall receive" (52). He goes to bed expecting to wake up cured, but finds that he is limping as usual. His uncle, not knowing precisely what Philip has hoped for, tells him that if his wishes did not come true it is because he has not had enough faith. Yet Philip does not see how he could show more: "If God had not cured him, it was because he did not really believe. And yet he did not see how he could believe more than he did" (55). Eventually, his thoughts turn to doubts: "presently the feeling came to him that . . . his faith would not be great enough. He could not resist the doubt that assailed him. He made his own experience into a general rule" (55). Thus, even before he officially becomes a student at King's, Philip becomes a skeptic in religion.

His skepticism turns almost to outright rejection by the time he reaches the point, several years later, when he must undergo his examinations for a scholarship to Oxford. It is understood that Philip will become a vicar, like his uncle, but he has other ideas. Partly because of his failed friendship with Rose, but more because he cannot imagine himself living the life of a vicar, Philip decides against competing for a place at the university. In doing so, he disappoints not only his uncle and aunt but also the headmaster of King's, Perkins, whom he especially admires.

Philip's refusal is based primarily on his firsthand observation of the life of his uncle in Blackstable: "As he grew up he had learned to know his uncle; Philip was downright and intolerant, and he could not understand that a man might sincerely say things as a clergyman which he never acted up to as a man. The deception outraged him. His uncle was a weak and selfish man, whose chief desire was to be saved trouble"

(82). The example of other vicars in other parishes in his corner of East Anglia does not present the matter any differently:

> There was not a soul for any of them to talk to except small farmers or fishermen; there were long winter evenings when the wind blew, whistling drearily through the leafless trees, and all around they saw nothing but the bare monotony of ploughed fields; and there was poverty, and there was lack of any work that seemed to matter; every kink in their characters had free play; there was nothing to restrain them; they grew narrow and eccentric; Philip knew all this, but in his young intolerance he did not offer it as an excuse. He shivered at the thought of living such a life; he wanted to get out into the world. (82–83)

Philip decides that, instead of Oxford, he wants to go to Germany to study for a short period of time. His choice stems partly from the background of his aunt, who was born in Germany, but also from a desire to study a modern language and to be exposed to new ideas, neither of which he expects to find at Oxford. Ultimately his will prevails in this matter, just as it did when he was a little boy wishing to play with his blocks on Sunday afternoon. He prevails over his uncle and his headmaster in achieving his goal, and the experience gives him a good feeling: "He felt a thrill of pride in his triumph. He had got his own way, and he was satisfied. His will had gained a victory over the wills of others" (88).

Philip, now approaching the point when he would have started an education leading to ordainment at one of the most prestigious universities in England, leaves for one of the oldest university towns in Europe to begin his *Lehrjahre*.

6

PHILIP CAREY'S *LEHRJAHRE:* FORMAL EDUCATION AND CHOICE OF PROFESSION

When Philip leaves England for Germany, he feels not only a personal sense of triumph, his will having prevailed over that of his uncle and his headmaster, but also a sense that his education is at last about to begin. In fact, one might say that Philip's entire story is one of his education, both in the formal sense of education for a profession and in the less formal sense of education in life. The formal part falls into three major phases: the year in Heidelberg, the two years in Paris, and the years at St. Luke's in London for medical school. The less formal aspect of his education continues throughout the book.

Philip's avowed purpose in going to Heidelberg is to study modern languages and generally to expose himself to new ideas. In both respects, his stay there is a success. Following a tutorial method not unlike that of the British universities, Philip studies Latin and German with Professor Erlin, the head of the household where he boards, French with Monsieur Ducroz, a Genevan who participated in revolutionary activities in France in the earlier part of the nineteenth century, and mathematics with an Englishman named Wharton who is taking a degree at the university. Wharton has adapted himself so well to the society of a German university town that he has trouble imagining himself returning to England at some point to teach. Ducroz is an embittered old man, a failed revolutionary, of the type that so often figures as a minor character in Maugham's short stories. Professor Erlin is almost a parody of a German academic type—highly conservative, hostile to new ideas—but he does convey to Philip his admiration for Goethe.

Ultimately, however, it is not from his tutors, interesting as they are, nor from the lectures he attends, but from several of his fellow boarders that Philip gains the greatest exposure to new ideas. Of particular importance in this respect are Weeks, an American theological student, and Hayward, an English aesthete. Weeks fuels Philip's doubts about religion and helps him reach the decision that it no longer means anything to him; Hayward introduces him to the notion that "truth is beauty, beauty truth." Both permanently influence his intellectual development, though no two people could be more different.

Weeks, a New Englander who is "cold and precise in his manner, a bloodless man, without passion" (108), nonetheless has a rapier-like wit and enjoys challenging Philip's conventional ideas and Hayward's supposedly unconventional ones. He is a Unitarian, which he defines as one who "very earnestly believes in almost everything that anybody else believes, and he has a very lively sustaining faith in he doesn't quite know what" (114). When Philip accuses him of making fun of his question as to what he believes, Weeks claims that he has arrived at his definition "after years of great labour and the most anxious, nerve-wracking study (114)."

Hayward, on the other hand, celebrates the pomp and circumstance of the Church of England and the Church of Rome: "I belong to the Church of England. But I love the gold and the silk which clothe the priest of Rome, and his celibacy, and the confessional, and purgatory; and in the darkness of an Italian cathedral, incense-laden and mysterious. I believe with all my heart in the miracle of the Mass" (112). He also believes, he soon adds, in "Aphrodite and Apollo and the Great God Pan," at which point Weeks suggests that he might as well throw in Buddhism and Mohammedanism, too.

Hayward responds to the ritual of religion, not to its substance, and though Philip defends Hayward to Weeks and regards Hayward as a friend, his own position on religion is soon closer to that of the American than that of the Englishman. Philip is shocked when he learns that Weeks (as a Unitarian) is a dissenter, but Weeks soon makes Philip realize that Philip's religion is based principally upon social class and circumstance—upon the vague sense that anyone other than high church is not really a gentleman. Through discussions with Weeks and also by attending mass with Hayward (where Philip realizes for the first time that if he had been born in the south of Germany he would likely be Roman Catholic), Philip is persuaded that religion is relative to class and geographical location. It is only a short step from this realization to the statement, in another conversation with Weeks: "I don't see why one should believe in God at all" (117).

At first, Philip is shocked by his own temerity in making such a statement. Later, alone, he thinks it through and comes to the conclusion that for him it is true:

> It was the most startling experience that he had ever had. He tried to think it all out; it was very exciting, since his whole life seemed concerned . . . and a mistake might lead to eternal damnation; but the more he reflected the more convinced he was; and though during the next few weeks he read books, aids to skepticism, with eager interest, it was only to confirm him in what he felt instinctively. The fact was that he had ceased to believe not for this reason or the other, but because he had not the religious temperament. Faith had been forced on him from the outside. It was a matter of environment and example. (117)

Weeks does not appeal to Philip personally but he has a permanent and generally positive influence on his thinking; Hayward does appeal to him as a friend and mentor, but his influence on his thinking is negative. Weeks, though engaged in the study of theology, is a realist; Hayward, on the other hand, is an idealist who believes that truth is revealed only through art. In the tug of war between realism and idealism that occurs in various forms throughout the novel, Maugham consistently comes down—at least until the very end—on the side of realism.

From the first Hayward is viewed as weak and ineffectual, a dreamer and dilettante who does not know how to act. Fraulein Anna, one of the Erlins' daughters, who is interested in how physiognomy reflects character (a study known as phrenology), remarks on the weakness of his jaw (104), and Weeks remarks again and again on the weakness of his thought. In his view of life, Hayward reflects the view of a whole generation, nurtured on the writings of major English aesthetes like John Ruskin (1819–1900) and Walter Pater (1839–94), who all believed, one way or another, that truth was found in beauty, the eternal verities in art. Hayward's one strength is his love of literature—"he could," Maugham writes, "impart his own passion with an admirable fluency" (108)—and he introduces Philip to a wide range of work previously unfamiliar to him, including Pater's *Marius the Epicurean* (1885), Meredith's *The Ordeal of Richard Feverel* (1859), and Gustave Flaubert's *Madame Bovary* (1857). But his influence, Maugham asserts, is pernicious, because he has no sense of reality:

> He was a man who saw nothing for himself, but only through a literary atmosphere, and he was dangerous because he had deceived himself into sincerity. He honestly mistook his sensuality for romantic emotion, his vacillation for the artistic temperament, and his idleness for philosophic calm. His mind, vulgar in its effort at refinement, saw everything a little larger than life size, with the outlines blurred, in a golden mist of sentimentality. He lied and never knew that he lied, and when it was pointed out to him said that lies were beautiful. He was an idealist. (121–22)

To the extent that Hayward contributes to Philip's inability to distinguish between the real and the ideal—a problem he faces throughout the novel—he is a dangerous companion.

When Philip returns to England he is precisely at the point in his life (approximately eighteen years of age) at which he should enter the university, but he has decided firmly, once and for all, that he will not attend Oxford. That possibility aside, Philip, as a gentleman, has four choices (and a possible fifth): "the Army, the Navy, the Law, and the Church" (139). Medicine, though not considered one hundred years ago quite the profession for a gentleman, is the fifth possibility, mainly because Philip's father was a surgeon. Philip has rejected the church, would need a university degree for the law, and has no inclination toward the military, nor, at this point in the novel, toward medicine. What remains?

The family solicitor recommends that he be apprenticed to a chartered accountant for a fee of three hundred pounds (half of which will be returned after one year if Philip decides he does not like the profession). Although his aunt and uncle doubt whether accountancy is an appropriate profession for a gentleman—indeed, whether it is a profession at all, since it comes so close to being a "trade"—in the end neither they nor Philip has much choice in the matter, since little else remains for him to do.

It is difficult at this point in the twentieth century to understand the hierarchy of professions that prevailed in England (and in Europe generally) during the last half of the nineteenth. The connection between a choice of profession and social class was so close, and the list of possibilities so narrowly prescribed, that one really had very few options to consider. Some professions now highly esteemed—such as acting and writing—were then considered highly disreputable (though half the peerage was having affairs with actresses or actors, and certain writers, such as Dickens, were considered national treasures). Other professions also now highly esteemed—such as medicine and accounting—were not very high in the pecking order. They were borderline activities that true gentlemen were likely to reject. Medicine could be profitable, but it was as likely to involve serving the poor. Accountancy, before the development of large corporations in the modern mode, was largely a matter of keeping the books in handwritten ledgers. Uriah Heep in Dickens's *David Copperfield* and Bob Cratchett in his *A Christmas Carol* show us as well as anything else the nature of accounting in the Victorian period.

Unfortunately, Philip, like many of his modern counterparts who decide to major in accounting now that it is a universally offered course of study, at least in American universities, finds that the profession is not for him. He is enticed partly by the possibility the apprenticeship affords him to live in London, but his year with Mr. Carter turns out to be perhaps the most miserable he has had since beginning at King's. He is very lonely, and he does not find his work very interesting. By the end of it he decides upon a dramatic change: he will go to Paris to study art.

His decision, which may surprise some readers, has as much to do with the city of Paris as it does with the practice of art. It also reflects the influence of Hayward and of a new friend, Emily Wilkinson, a governess who has lived in France and with whom Philip has his first affair. In Germany, Philip did watercolors that were much admired, and he has always had an eye for art. During his lonely year in London, art galleries provide him with a pastime. He has been encouraged by Hayward ("My feeling," he writes him in a letter, quoting Pater, "is that one should look upon life as an adventure, one should burn with the hard, gem-like flame, and one should take risks, one should expose oneself to danger. Why do you not go to Paris and study art? I always thought you had talent" [168]), and by Miss Wilkinson, who lends him a copy of Mürger's *La Vie de Bohème*, the source for Puccini's popular opera *La Bohème*, about life among art students in the Latin Quarter.

A visit toward the end of that year to Paris with a senior associate at the accounting firm however, is what really turns Philips's thoughts to the study of art:

> He was all eyes as the train sped through the country [from Calais]; he adored the sand dunes, their color seemed to him more lovely than anything he had ever seen; and he was enchanted with the canals and the long lines of poplars. When they got out of the Gare du Nord, and trundled along the cobbled streets in a ramshackle, noisy cab, it seemed to him that he was breathing a new air so intoxicating that he could hardly restrain himself from shouting aloud. (169)

Philip determines to himself, "This is the real thing," and makes plans to withdraw from his apprenticeship and go to Paris.

Once again, however, he encounters opposition from his uncle. The vicar is certain that Philip merely wants to indulge himself and refuses to approve an allowance. Philip toys with the idea of pawning his father's gold watch and chain, as well as some jewelry, to put together enough money to go; the greater his uncle's resistance, the stronger Philip's determination to follow through on his idea. In the end he is saved by his

Aunt Louisa, who has put aside a few hundred pounds that she insists he take. With this money, he continues his education in the City of Light.

Philip's enthusiasm for France was shared by his creator. Maugham was born there, coming to England at the age of ten when his father died. He spent time in France intermittently from the time he became a published author, in 1897, until 1926, when he bought a house on the French Riviera and settled there for most of the rest of his life. (During World War II he lived in the United States.) In most respects France was more home to Maugham than England was. He was bilingual, having learned French as a child, and in many ways he had more sympathy with French culture than with English. It was no accident that one of his volumes of short stories was called *Cosmopolitans,* nor that he chose so often to write about exiles.

About art he had an equal degree of enthusiasm. Although he neither studied art nor practiced it as an amateur, he appreciated it from very early in his life. He was a close friend of the painter Gerald Kelly, who was to do Maugham's portrait many times, and he began collecting art seriously in the late 'teens, when, during a trip to Tahiti, he acquired a door panel painted by Paul Gauguin. Toward the end of his life his collection of French impressionist art was extremely valuable and brought high prices at auction. He also wrote frequently about artists and art, most notably in his novel *The Moon and Sixpence* (1919), based on Gauguin's life, and in such books as *Don Fernando* (1935), which contains a memorable essay on El Greco.

When Philip went to Paris in the 1890s to study art, it was truly the capital of the art world. It was to remain so until well into the twentieth century. In Paris, more than any place else, modern art was born, and because the Paris chapters of *Of Human Bondage* deal with this subject, it is worth considering for a moment. What were the prevailing tendencies in art during the 1890s? What artists did Philip and his friends consider important? Whom did they wish to emulate in their own work? "They talked of a thousand things, and they all talked at once. No one paid the smallest attention to anyone else. They talked of the places they had been to in the summer, of studios, of the various schools; they mentioned names which were unfamiliar to Philip: Monet, Manet, Renoir, Pisarro,

Degas. Philip listened with all his ears, and though he felt a little out of it, his heart leaped with exultation" (181). Thus Maugham describes Philip's first encounter with his Paris friends, Clutton, Flanagan, and Lawson.

The names they mention are among the leading artists of the impressionist group, which by the mid-1880s had become the acknowledged leader of French art.[12] Philip, whose taste in art has been shaped by Hayward and by his own wanderings in the National Gallery and other museums in London, does not know the work of these artists. From the vantage point of today (or even from that of 1913 or 1914, when Maugham was writing), we can see that Philip's friends were on to something when they said that Manet's *Olympia* will someday hang in the Louvre and that it will be esteemed as highly as Ingres's *Odalisque*.

The fledgling artist of the late nineteenth century in France faced an art world of clearly defined spheres of interest. On the one hand, there was the art of the academy, represented by such artists as Carolus Duran and Bouguereau, the teacher of Degas, who espoused the traditional virtues of studio art. These included drawing from the model as Philip does at Amitrano's, copying the work of masters in the Louvre, and other activities thought essential to the training of an artist. Admission to this society ultimately depended upon one's success at the annual salons, which represented a form of official recognition of artistic accomplishment, the inner sanctum of the French art world.

On the other hand, the impressionists asked the artist to come outdoors, to paint nature or city scenes as they really appeared to the human eye, with a brushstroke and palette radically different from those of more academic painters. The aim of the impressionists was to represent light more accurately than previous artists had represented it. Their work, however, did not appear more realistic to most of its first viewers, who saw it as a sketch, or impression, of reality, hence the name *impressionism*.

Philip's taste in painting, while not utterly traditional, nevertheless seems conservative to his new friends. He values highly the work of certain English artists associated with the Pre-Raphaelite group. To aesthetes like Hayward, the art of the Pre-Raphaelites (led by poet-painter Dante Gabriel Rossetti, 1828–82) represents the forefront of artistic activity; to Philip's Paris friends, such work seems literary, tainted by Victorian moralism and unpainterly values. Philip soon buys a postcard of the *Olympia* and hangs it on his wall along with the *Odalisque* of Ingres. His tastes change under the influence of a new environment and new friends.

Of Philip's associates, several show genuine talent. Lawson shows promise enough to look forward to a future as a portrait painter. Clutton, eccentric and original, has possibly the greatest talent of them all, but the most difficulty in finding a way to express it. Ruth Chalice and the American Flanagan are at least competent painters. Technically, all of them have skills that Philip, a beginner, lacks when he goes to Paris. In a sense, his education at Amitrano's is the slow, gradual acquiring of the technical skills needed to draw and paint.

One of his fellow students at Amitrano's lacks these skills, though she has persevered for years with the notion that she will be an artist. This is Fanny Price. In many ways, what happens to Fanny has more influence on Philip's artistic career than anything else that happens to him in Paris.

Like Hayward, Fanny is an idealist, but one who works to fulfill an impossible goal. Homely and unhealthy looking, she has studied at Amitrano's for some time without making any progress. Yet she is convinced that she will be an artist and earn her living by her art. She attaches herself to Philip and, though he has ambivalent feelings about her, he gradually becomes concerned for her welfare.

Whatever delusions Fanny Price has about her artistic ability should be dashed by the master, Foinet, once noted for his landscapes. He tells her plainly that she has no talent: "It is my duty to tell you that you are wasting your time. It would not matter that you have no talent, talent does not run about the streets in these days, but you have not the beginning of an aptitude. How long have you been here? A child of five after two lessons would draw better than you do" (196). Although Fanny seems to lose none of her resolution after this attack, her suicide provides the final answer. That pathetic event—along with the example of another misguided artist, the Spaniard Miguel Ajuria, who badly wants to write and writes badly—leads Philip to seek the advice of Foinet about his own work.

That advice, given after the master casts a cold eye on everything Philip has done, is pointed and honest: "If you were to ask my advice, I should say: take your courage in both hands and try your luck at something else. It sounds very hard, but let me tell you this: I would give all I have in the world if someone had given me that advice when I was your age and I had taken it" (248).

Foinet and Fanny are two of the most memorable minor characters in a book filled with them, and they represent as clearly as any other characters the polarities of realism and idealism that Philip, in his growth and development as an individual, is constantly confronting. Monsieur Foinet, sad and embittered though he may be, looks at the world more realistically than Fanny Price and thus falls into that small group of characters who perceives the world as it is.

The poet Cronshaw, also a major influence on Philip during his Paris years, represents an interesting case of a character who is part realist, part idealist. In the abstract, his advice is often excellent and gives the novel one of its major metaphors. In the concrete, his life is largely a waste, and his talent as a poet is small.

But it is Cronshaw who suggests to Philip that one must search constantly for the meaning of life, that there is no single meaning. "Have you been to the Cluny, the museum?" he asks Philip at one point. "There you will see Persian carpets of the most exquisite hue and of a pattern the beautiful intricacy of which delights and amazes the eye. In them you will see the mystery and the sensual beauty of the East. . . . You were asking just now what was the meaning of life. Go and look at those Persian carpets, and one of these days the answer will come to you" (213). The pursuit of that answer occupies Philip to the very end of the novel.

Philip does not wish to be a second-rate artist, nor a starving one. Monsieur Foinet's advice on that matter also touches home: "Money is like a sixth sense without which you cannot make a complete use of the other five" (248). Rather than end up like Cronshaw, spending his nights in an alcoholic stupor and his days trying to write reviews or do whatever is necessary to make ends meet; rather than end up like Fanny Price, hanging from a rope in her attic apartment, dead of starvation and despair—rather than follow such desperate and hopeless paths, Philip will return to England and do something else. The death of his Aunt Louisa, after his second year in Paris, provides the occasion.

Philip is now in his majority and in charge of his own fortunes. His uncle has the opinion that he should become a doctor, and Philip agrees. He makes this choice partly because his father had been a doctor, but "chiefly because it was an occupation which seemed to give a good deal of personal freedom" (255). Thus, almost randomly, the matter is decided. After two years in Paris, one year of apprenticeship in London, and one year in Heidelberg, Philip, now twenty-one, decides to begin his medical training in London at his father's old hospital, St. Luke's. In a sense, as Philip thinks later on, the practice of medicine has much in common with the practice of art: "There was humanity in the rough, the materials the artist worked on; and Philip felt a curious thrill when it occurred to him that he was in the position of the artist and the patients were like clay in his hands" (399).

Maugham himself had been a medical student, enrolled at the somewhat younger age of eighteen at St. Thomas's Hospital in London. (Maugham's father had been a lawyer with the British embassy in Paris, not a surgeon.) His reasons for choosing to study medicine may well have been the same as Philip's—"personal freedom"—but in the end Maugham never practiced. At the point he might have begun, he published *Liza of Lambeth*, his first novel, based in part on his experiences as a medical student with the London poor, and embarked on a literary career. All of his experiences in medical school, however, play an important part in his description of Philip's progress through St. Luke's, and the reader may assume that Philip's experiences are more or less typical.

Less typical, one hopes, are the personal experiences that accompany Philip's medical education, for it is at this point in the novel, as Philip enters the final phase of his formal education, that his most painful education in love is about to begin. By chance, in a London restaurant, he meets the woman who is to make his life hell for the next several years.

7

PHILIP'S SEXUALITY

By chapter LV of *Of Human Bondage*, when Philip Carey meets Mildred Rogers for the first time, he has just entered into the final phase of his formal education. As a new student at medical school, he has few friends and is passing through the inevitable period of adjustment that comes with the beginning of a new endeavor. He has been in art school for the past several years, not a place where one is examined on facts and details, and he now faces a long course of memorization and frequent examinations. He also faces, once again, a large city where he previously had lived an unhappy life. Although he is more equal to the test of such a life than he would have been several years before, he is still far from being a fully developed person.

In chapter LIII, Philip had reviewed his life to date and concluded that there were three things important "to find out: man's relation to the world he lives in, man's relation with the men among whom he lives, and finally man's relation to himself" (258). Philip has begun to reach some conclusion on the first of these points, but on the other two he has a long way to go. In the end, to find the meaning in the carpet of Cronshaw's parable (260), he must do more: he must work out his relation with the women among whom he lives as well as the men; then, and only then, will

he come to some understanding of himself. As the title of the novel suggests, Philip's process of learning will not be easy.

With this in mind, perhaps it is fitting that Philip's first reaction to
Mildred is a kind of physical revulsion. As Maugham describes her, there
is little for him to feel excited about:

> She had the small regular features, the blue eyes, and the broad low
> brow which the Victorian painters, Lord Leighton, Alma Tadema, and
> a hundred others, induced the world they lived in to accept as a type of
> Greek beauty. She seemed to have a great deal of hair; it was arranged
> with peculiar elaboration and done over the forehead in what she
> called an Alexandra fringe. She was very anaemic. Her thin lips were
> pale, and her skin was delicate, of a faint green colour, without a touch
> of red even in the cheeks. She had very good teeth. She took great pains
> to prevent her work from spoiling her hands, and they were small, thin,
> and white. She went about her duties with a bored look. (267–68)

Mildred has made herself look like the pictures of fashionable
women in newspapers and magazines (the Alexandra fringe was named
for a hair style popularized by the wife of the Prince of Wales, Queen
Victoria's son, who was soon to become Edward VII). In her coloring,
however, Mildred is almost corpse-like and definitely unappealing. She is
also "tall and thin, with narrow hips and the chest of a boy" (267), and
with such a form no one, Philip says, would look at her in Paris.

If Mildred's appearance is none too appealing in spite of her obvious
care for herself and her fine teeth (less common in the late nineteenth
century than today), her manner is what puts Philip and his friend off
more than her appearance. Most waitresses try to be at least moderately
cheerful toward their customers, if only because their income depends
on it. Mildred, however, is rude. She sees Philip and Dunsford as students
and therefore of very little consequence. "I'm here to take orders and to
wait on customers," she tells them curtly. "I've got nothing to say to
them, and I don't want them to say anything to me" (269).

Philip dislikes Mildred's manner but, all the same, finds himself
coming back to the restaurant. He makes up a story to keep his friend
from coming along, and, "not a little ashamed of his weakness" (269), he

returns after a few days, only to be snubbed again. Try as he might, he can't get her out of his mind: "It was absurd to care what an anaemic little waitress said to him; but he was strangely humiliated" (270). He argues ineffectually with the urge to return for more, but return he does.

This time Mildred recognizes him and talks with him at least a little. He is helped by a drawing he does of her one day, as, between customers, she sits reading. She is obviously pleased by the attention but doesn't thank him. In fact, she seems much more interested in Philip's friend than she does in Philip, and definitely more interested in an older man, a German named Miller, whom Dunsford has noticed her talking to before.

Just as Philip thinks he is making some headway with Mildred, he finds Miller in the restaurant one day, and Mildred pays Philip no attention. He is furious, yet he comes back the next day and asks her to go with him to the theater. After this first excursion, it suddenly comes to him that he is in love with her. He can scarcely believe it:

> He had thought of love as a rapture which seized one so that all the world seemed spring-like, he had looked forward to an ecstatic happiness; but this was not happiness; it was a hunger of the soul, it was a painful yearning, it was a bitter anguish he had never known before. He tried to think when it had first come to him. He did not know. He only remembered that each time he had gone into the shop, after the first two or three times, it had been with a little feeling in the heart that was pain; and he remembered that when she spoke to him he felt curiously breathless. When she left him it was wretchedness and when she came to him again it was despair. (278)

In this manner, with the pattern of encouragement and rejection, Philip begins the relationship that dominates the middle and later chapters of the book and that, more than any other portrayed, forms his future character.

What relationships does Philip have with women before Mildred? Before considering in detail his relationship with the waitress who makes his life so miserable, it is useful to consider his previous relationships with women and their meaning to him. The first of these is with the friend of his uncle's who encourages him to go to Germany and then later to Paris, Emily Wilkinson.

In novels of initiation it is often an older woman who introduces a young man to sexual love. And so, to some extent at least, it is with Philip Carey. Until the time he meets Miss Wilkinson, his love affairs have been merely fantasies. With her, he has first real affair, though whether their affair is fully consummated is a matter of opinion.

Miss Wilkinson is the daughter of a clergyman, though she does not dress like one. Clergymen's daughters, Philip remarks, usually wore "ill-cut clothes and stout boots" (131), chiefly black in color. They did everything they could to look plain and unfeminine, considering feminine graces to be inappropriate for women so close to the cloth. Miss Wilkinson, on the other hand, dresses showily and is heavily powdered, a fact that Philip finds somewhat embarrassing. In appearance she is likened to a bird: "She had large black eyes and her nose was slightly aquiline; in profile she had somewhat the look of a bird of prey, but full face she was prepossessing" (131). Her age is somewhat indeterminate, but Philip knows she is older than he is. She is also extremely flirtatious, and it is not long, during her summer visit to Blackstable in the interlude between Philip's year in Heidelberg and his apprenticeship in accountancy in London, till they begin to become more intimate.

Miss Wilkinson fuels Philip's ardor with stories of her love affairs in Paris, and he begins to think it might be interesting to have an affair with her. It is a sort of game to him, saying romantic things to her, "the most thrilling game he had ever played; and the wonderful thing was that he felt almost all he said" (146). Everything he had ever read on the subject comes to his aid, and secretively, in romantic fashion (because, quite obviously, Philip's uncle and aunt would take a dim view of the whole thing), they contrive to meet in the garden and take walks together alone.

Finally, the moment of truth arrives. Having flirted for weeks and repeated all the romantic phrases, Philip finds himself alone in the house with Miss Wilkinson. It is his plan for them to culminate their affair, but he has cold feet: "He felt sick with apprehension. He wished with all his heart that he had not suggested the plan; but it was too late now; he must take the opportunity which he had made. What would Miss Wilkinson think of him if he did not!" (148).

He stands trembling outside her door and then finally, having waited as long as he possibly can, turns the door handle and goes in. She is standing there in her petticoat and camisole (a loose-fitting undergarment, like a slip). In this pose she is most unappealing: "She looked grotesque. Philip's heart sank as he stared at her; she had never seemed so unattractive; but it was too late now" (149).

What happens after the door closes behind him? The question is not prurient; the reader needs to know, in order to interpret Philip's later experiences with Mildred and with other women in the novel. The chapter ends as Philip closes the door and the next chapter begins the following morning as he wakes up, thinking that now he should call Miss Wilkinson Emily. Certainly her behavior to him suggests that she is in love; his to her that something has happened and he wishes that it hadn't. In general, from this point on, Miss Wilkinson becomes to Philip a burden that he is only too anxious to shed.

At the same time, however, when he gets to Paris several chapters later and begins the study of art, Maugham tells us that Philip, confronted with a model on his first day at Amitrano's, "had never seen a naked woman before" (178). Does this mean that Emily Wilkinson did not remove her petticoat and camisole? If she did, is it possible that Philip, finding her grotesque, simply doesn't look at her naked body?

Having sex with at least some clothing on is not unusual, then or now, despite what one sees in the movies. Philip's modesty is not strange, either, given the nature of his relationship with Miss Wilkinson and his own inexperience. Perhaps it is enough to say that Maugham seems to want us to think that Philip has lost his virginity to Miss Wilkinson in their one night together and then, because she wants to turn that event into a long-standing relationship, increasingly regrets the experience later on. And even if Miss Wilkinson did choose to remove her undergarments for her young lover, it is doubtful under the circumstances that he would have studied her body.

The key element in their relationship is its unreality: it is a literary love affair that, when it does become real, loses its vitality for Philip. In this sense, it is another case of the problem of the real and the ideal, of the one inevitably not measuring up to the other. The more impassioned the letters Miss Wilkinson sends him, the less he feels inclined to reply. He is happy she is in Berlin and does nothing to encourage her to come to see him in Paris. By then, at any rate, he has found new friends, including one who has made him the focus of her attention.

At the time Philip receives Fanny Price's message and then discovers her body, he realizes fully for the first time what he must have meant to her: "Please come at once when you get this. I couldn't put up with it any more. Please come yourself. I can't bear the thought that anyone else should touch me. I want you to have everything" (232). Among her few possessions Philip finds a piece of paper on which his name is written over and over. It comes to him as a shock that Fanny cared so much about him: "if she had . . . , why did she not let him help her? He would so gladly have done all he could. He felt remorseful because he had refused to see that she looked upon him with any particular feeling" (234).

Unfortunately, the feeling that Fanny has for Philip is completely one-sided. The best that Philip can return is a certain amount of pity, which is only strengthened by what ultimately happens to Fanny. Her death serves as a lesson to him—it teaches the danger of self-delusion, of believing that one has talent when in fact one doesn't. Her suicide reminds him forcibly of the fate of so many others like her: "The history of painting was full of artists who had earned nothing at all. He must resign himself to penury; and it was worthwhile if he produced work which was immortal; but he had a terrible fear that he would never be more than second-rate" (240).

Fanny cares for Philip, but what she feels is not passionate love; it is a desire to be recognized, to have someone care about her. In a way it is a selfish and neurotic form of caring, as remote from real love as Fanny is remote from the real world. No less unreal, but completely different in emotional direction, is Philip's attachment to Ruth Chalice.

Ruth Chalice is in some ways typical of a sort who belonged to the Bohemian circle in Paris and preferred life among artists to the *vie ordinaire*. But Ruth is more than just a hanger-on; in addition to being a good conversationalist and companion, she also has some talent with a brush.

With Ruth, Philip is slow to recognize his feelings for what they are, and, when he finally does, it is too late. By then she has already made a commitment to Lawson.

"With her large brown eyes, thin, ascetic face, her pale skin, and broad forehead, she might have stepped out of a picture by Burne-Jones" (220)—thus, Maugham describes Ruth Chalice in terms similar to those used in describing Mildred Rogers later in the novel. As a would-be artist, Philip might be expected to look at the world through painting, but it is also true that a woman like Ruth Chalice would be likely to make herself look like the popular work of the day. With her "romantic air" and her nature "wantonly aesthetic," she is both attractive and somewhat intimidating to Philip.

In the summer, near the forest of Fontainebleau, he realizes just how much he is attracted to her: "He felt himself a fool not to have seen that she was attractive. He thought he detected in her a touch of contempt for him, because he had not had the sense to see that she was there, in his way, and in Lawson a suspicion of superiority" (225). He can imagine himself in Ruth's arms, but it is Lawson who in fact is there; in her presence, he is aware of her defects as much as her good qualities. "Would he always love only in absence," he asks himself, "and be prevented from enjoying anything when he had the chance by that deformity of vision which seemed to exaggerate the revolting?" (226).

Except for Fanny and Ruth, the women in Philip's Paris are prostitutes, "stray amours," to whom he is introduced by his friend Flanagan. He thinks of these encounters as " . . . sly visits to houses in a *cul-de-sac*, with the drawingroom in Utrecht velvet, and the mercenary graces of painted women" (225). How frequently Philip avails himself of the services of prostitutes is not clear (he is obviously limited to some extent by his lack of money), but prostitution was widespread in the late nineteenth century, both in Paris and in London, and for young men of all classes was a source of sexual release. It is clear that for Philip it provides no emotional satisfaction.

By the time he meets Mildred Rogers, then, Philip has had a limited amount of sexual experience and no real emotional commitment to any relationship with a woman other than his mother and his aunt.

Small wonder he is struck so strongly by the irony of feeling "a bitter anguish he had never known before" and recognizing that the source of his feeling is an anemic-looking waitress who seems to have no real feeling for him.

Philip's relationship with Mildred passes through several distinct phases during the several years of his emotional bondage. The first phase takes him from his first meeting with her in the restaurant to the point, in chapter LXIII, when she tells him she is going to marry Miller. The second begins with her return after Miller abandons her when she becomes pregnant (chapter LXIX) and includes the birth of baby and her affair with Philip's friend Griffiths. The final phase begins with Philip's discovery that Mildred is supporting herself by prostitution and ends with the episode in which Mildred willfully destroys his possessions and leaves him for the last time (chapter XCVII). Except for one final brief meeting, when Philip realizes that Mildred has venereal disease (chapter CIX), they never meet again.

From the beginning of their relationship, a basic pattern asserts itself and only grows stronger with the passage of time. Philip feels humiliated by his attraction to Mildred and wants the relationship to end, but, in spite of himself, comes back for more. Mildred, on the other hand, is not attracted to Philip but, out of convenience and then economic necessity, keeps coming back for his support. She uses him without ever giving him more than the slightest indication that she cares about him; he seems to enjoy being used by her and, throughout much of their relationship, expects almost nothing in return. Philip does not want to love, but to suffer.

Maugham's language from the beginning emphasizes Philip's need to endure pain. The passage at the end of chapter LVII has already been noted, with its reference to "painful yearning" and "bitter anguish." At the beginning of the very next chapter, vacillating between returning to the restaurant and not returning, Philip decides he must go and "hating himself, he went" (279). Later in the same chapter, he wants "to hurt her as much as she was hurting him" (284) and then, when it seems that Mildred might actually leave him, "he was willing to forget everything, he was ready for any humiliation" (284). By chapter LIX the theme becomes more explicit:

> He loved the woman so that he knew he had never loved before. He did not mind her faults of person or of character, he thought he loved them too: at all events they meant nothing to him. It did not seem himself that was concerned; he felt that he had been seized by some strange force that moved him against his will, contrary to his interests; and because he had a passion for freedom he hated the chains which bound him. He laughed at himself when he thought how often he had longed to experience the overwhelming passion. He cursed himself because he had given way to it. (286)

Preoccupied with his obsession, Philip neglects his studies and fails his biology examination. In his embarrassment, he wants to avoid his fellow students, among whom the sole topic of conversation will be the recent exam. Rather than avoid them, however, he joins them at tea-time because "he wanted to inflict suffering upon himself. . . . there must have been some strange morbidity in his nature which made him take a grim pleasure in self-torture" (289).

In a paroxysm of self-abasement trying to persuade Mildred to love him shortly before she announces her engagement to Miller, he appeals to her sympathies in the crudest possible way, by saying that she probably cannot love him because he is a cripple. "It made him feel almost sick," Maugham writes, "to utter the words" (297), but utter them he does.

In clinical terms, Philip suffers from masochism—the desire to suffer pain, to feel humiliated or debased. Sex researchers Masters and Johnson define the condition tersely in their textbook on human sexuality: "The need for experiencing pain and humiliation in order to achieve sexual gratification."[13] This urge is expressed in various ways, from the actual to the symbolic; one need not experience pain literally to qualify as a masochist: mental torture causes as much suffering as physical. In pornographic literature, however, the torture is usually physical and involves the use of chains and whips. When sado-masochistic urges are expressed in this form, they are known as bondage, another possible source for the title of the novel.

Whether symbolic or real, masochistic urges represent a sexual disorder, and, on the evidence of the text of *Of Human Bondage*, Philip suffers from precisely such a problem. Although he suffers direct physical pain only once in his relationship with Mildred (when his hand encounters a pin at her waist, placed there to discourage men from putting an "arm where it's got no business to be" [293]), he suffers mental anguish over and over again, sometimes to the point where distinguishing it from physical suffering is difficult. He also seems unable to resist experiencing more humiliation. In so doing, he acts against his will, which philosophically he has determined to be the most important human element. Once again the real and the ideal are in conflict in Philip; in the ideal he asserts the power of the will, but in the real situation of his relationship with Mildred he is powerless.

Philip also seems to suffer to some extent from another form of sexual pathology, known as voyeurism: "A sexual variation," Masters and Johnson define it, "in which a person obtains sexual gratification by witnessing the sexual acts of others or by spying on them when they are undressing or nude."[14] Once again, as with his masochism, Philip's voyeurism is symbolic; he does not literally wish to watch the sexual act performed, but he does want to create the opportunity for Mildred to be involved sexually with someone else. At the same time, he hates himself for having such desires.

This aspect of Philip's sexual character perhaps shows itself first, in nascent form, during the years in France, when he takes his vacation with Ruth Chalice and Lawson. During that summer, when he becomes aware that Ruth and Lawson have become lovers, he is envious of Lawson and jealous, "not of the individual concerned, but of his love. He wished that he was standing in his shoes and feeling with his heart. He was troubled, and the fear seized him that love would pass him by" (225).

With Mildred, the voyeuristic desire becomes gradually more explicit as their relationship deepens. Toward the end of its first phase, Mildred makes Philip furious by accepting an invitation to dinner and a show from someone else. In the end, however, he can't persuade her not to go and ultimately follows her to observe her with the other man: "Philip went to the Tivoli and saw Mildred with her companion, a

smooth-faced young man with sleek hair and the spruce look of a commercial traveler. . . . Mildred wore a black picture hat with ostrich feath-
ers in it, which became her well. She was listening to her host with that
quiet smile which Philip knew" (298).

The culmination of Philip's voyeuristic urges comes during the second phase of their relationship, with the affair between Mildred and
Philip's friend Griffiths. Griffiths, a fellow medical student, has nursed
Philip through a bout of influenza; Philip, in turn, has helped Mildred
through her pregnancy and the placement of her baby with a woman in
the country. When Mildred returns to London, Philip invites Griffiths to
join them for dinner. When Griffiths appears in his rooms Philip is struck
by his physical appearance: "He was a handsome creature, tall and thin;
his head was placed well on the body, it gave him a conquering air which
was attractive; and his curly hair, his bold, friendly blue eyes, his red
mouth, were charming. Philip saw Mildred look at him with appreciation, and he felt a curious satisfaction" (359). From this point on, Philip,
at once thrilled by the prospect and appalled by it, watches the two come
closer and closer together until their affair reaches its climax.

Mildred is obviously taken by Griffiths from the first, showing more
enthusiasm and spirit than Philip has seen in her for months. Philip, ob-
serving Mildred's obvious interest and Griffiths's sensuous appeal, begins to see himself in a special role: "He admired them both so much that
it seemed natural enough for them to admire one another. He did not
care if Griffiths absorbed Mildred's attention, he would have her to himself during the evening; he had something of the attitude of a loving husband, confident in his wife's affection, who looks on with amusement
while she flirts harmlessly with a stranger" (361).

His detached attitude does not last long. After yet another dinner
together, Philip is seized by a violent fit of jealousy when he realizes in
the cab that Griffiths is holding Mildred's hand. This feeling gives way
soon, however, to a desire to test them even further: "A strange desire to
torture himself seized him, and he got up, saying he wanted to go and
drink something. Mildred and Griffiths had never been alone together
for a moment. He wanted to leave them by themselves" (362). Now his

masochistic and voyeuristic urges come together as he observes the two of them from a distance.

> He was throwing them together now to make the pain he suffered more intolerable. He did not go to the bar, but up into the balcony, from where he could watch them and not be seen. They had ceased to look at the stage and were smiling into one another's eyes. Griffiths was talking with his usual happy fluency and Mildred seemed to hang on his lips. Philip's head began to ache frightfully. He stood there motionless. He knew he would be in the way if he went back. They were enjoying themselves without him, and he was suffering, suffering. (363)

Philip has planned for some time a trip to Paris with Mildred, but as she grows more infatuated with Griffiths she does not want to go. Instead, she and Griffiths, who has declared his love for her in a letter, plan a weekend at Oxford, where he attended the university, and Philip ends up providing the funds for the trip: "He had a fiendish desire to break down their scruples, he wanted to know how abominably they could behave towards him; if he tempted them a little more they would yield, and he took a fierce joy at the thought of their dishonour. Though every word tortured him, he found in the torture a horrible delight" (375).

After they leave, taking Philip's money for the trip, he spends the day alone and gets drunk: "He could not go to bed, he knew he would not sleep, and he dreaded the pictures which his vivid imagination would place before him" (378–79). In the end, Philip's worst fears are realized when Mildred and Griffiths run away together after their weekend. Once again, Mildred has used him; once again, he swears not to see her again.

The affair between Mildred and Griffiths does have one positive effect. Even though Philip takes Mildred in one more time and she once more deals with him ruinously, Philip no longer feels the same degree of emotional attachment toward her as he did during the second phase of their relationship. In fact, during the final phase he remains emotionally detached from her. He no longer wants to kiss her nor debase himself as he did before. The difference is due partly to Philip's exposure to Thorpe Athelny and his family, and to the effect this exposure has on his view of life.

Less obvious than Philip's tendency toward masochistic and voyeuristic behavior, but nonetheless important to an interpretation of his sexual character, is the evidence in the text of his homosexual urges. These urges show themselves first, as noted previously, during his adolescence at Tercanbury and later in reference to Griffiths. In neither case do they result in overt homosexual behavior, but the evidence of such emotions on Philip's part is so strong that it requires special notice. It forms a kind of subtheme in the story that perhaps sheds additional light on Philip's strange behavior toward Griffiths and Mildred.

At Tercanbury, where Philip has few friends and keeps for the most part to himself, he frequently identifies himself with boys who are better looking and sounder of body: "He took to a singular habit. He would imagine that he was some boy whom he had a particular fancy for; he would throw his soul, as it were, into the other's body, talk with his voice and laugh with his laugh; he would imagine himself doing all the things the other did. It was so vivid that he seemed for a moment really to be no longer himself" (72). When he is befriended by Rose, it is as if his fantasies suddenly become real.

Rose is not especially handsome, but "his eyes were charming, and when he laughed (he was constantly laughing) his face wrinkled all round them in a jolly way" (73). At his glance, Maugham writes, "Philip felt a curious tremor in his heart" (73). Rose is a popular boy, in contrast with Philip, and friendship with him means acceptance by boys who had previously rejected him. However, Philip seeks "a more exclusive attachment" and claims "as a right what before he had accepted as a favour" (75). His possessiveness drives Rose away, and soon he is lonely again.

This relationship, with its homoerotic overtones, is typical of the kind of schoolboy friendships that proliferated in Maugham's day in the English public schools. Were the evidence of homosexual leanings on Philip's part to end with this episode, little would be established about his character beyond the fact that something typical happened. When he meets Griffiths, however, he is no longer a schoolboy; he is in his twenties and has entered into the adult sphere of experience. He has also had at least a limited amount of experience with women. Nonetheless, some of

the passages of the novel in which Griffiths figures suggest that Philip is
sexually attracted to him.

In chapter LXVIII, as Philip comes down with a bout of influenza
and Griffiths nurses him through it, Philip responds to Griffiths's min-
istrations. We know that Griffiths is handsome and has sensuous appeal; what these descriptive details show us is Philip's response to
these qualities.

When Griffiths first appears in Philip's rooms to see how he is,
Philip's response is to blush, "he knew not why" (325). Griffiths minis-
ters to Philip just as he would if he were in a hospital, including washing him
when Philip is "too weak and wretched to resist" (327). Compare the description of Philip's feelings when he realizes he is emotionally bound to
Mildred: "He felt just as he had felt sometimes in the hands of a bigger
boy at school. He had struggled against the superior strength till his own
strength was gone, and he was rendered quite powerless—he remembered the peculiar languor he had felt in his limbs, almost as though he
were paralyzed—so that he could not help himself at all" (286). Philip is
"deeply touched by the feminine tenderness of this strong young man"
and "worshipped him as at school he had worshipped boys who were tall
and straight and high of spirits" (328).

Certainly Philip's feelings for Griffiths go beyond mere gratitude. In
bringing together Griffiths and Mildred, Philip is also encouraging
Griffiths—whom he admires and would emulate—to take over his role
in relationship to Mildred. There is no evidence anywhere in the text that
the affair between Philip and Mildred, no matter how prolonged nor
how intense his feelings, is ever consummated physically. Mildred gets
what she wants from Griffiths, and Philip knows that she does.

If the text suggests that Philip responds sensuously to Griffiths, it
also suggests that part of Mildred's physical appeal to Philip is that she
looks like a boy. Ted Morgan has pointed out the emphasis Maugham
gives to the boy-like quality of her features ("She was tall and thin, with
narrow hips and the chest of a boy" [267]). She is also said to have a kind
of Greek beauty popularized by Victorian painters, in whose work an-
drogyny (the fusion of male and female sexual characteristics) was common. It is even possible, as Morgan also suggests, that in the story of

Philip and Mildred Maugham is describing in disguised form an affair with a young man.[15]

These speculations on the matter of Philip's sexual identity mean more if viewed against the background of sexual confusion in Maugham's own life. There is every reason to see relationships between Maugham's life and his novel—in his foreword Maugham encourages the reader to see them—and in some cases the relationships are so close that the characters' real-life counterparts can be named. The original of Etheridge Hayward, for example, was Ellingham Brooks, whom Maugham met in Heidelberg in 1890 and with whom he had his first homosexual affair. Knowing that Hayward's original was homosexual adds something to passages such as this:

> Sometimes Hayward left Philip to go home by himself. He would never exactly reply to Philip's eager questioning, but with a merry, rather stupid laugh, hinted at a romantic amour; he quoted a few lines of Rossetti, and once showed Philip a sonnet in which passion and purple, pessimism and pathos, were packed together on the subject of a young lady called Trude. Hayward surrounded his sordid and vulgar little adventures with a glow of poetry, and thought he touched hands with Pericles and Phidias because to describe the object of his attentions he used the word *hetaira*. . . . (120–21)

Homosexuality was commonly known during the Victorian era as Greek love, and it is not difficult to imagine how Brooks's encounters with male pick-ups have been transformed in this passage into adventures with women.

Throughout the first four-and-a-half decades of his life, Maugham led essentially a bisexual existence. At the very moment he made a commitment to marriage for the first time (to Syrie Barnardo, later famous as a decorator), he also met and fell in love with the man he was to live with for most of his life, Gerald Haxton. Maugham lived between two loves and two modes of existence, seemingly unable to resolve the two (in much the same way that Philip Carey is drawn continually to Mildred in spite of his intentions to do otherwise). Ultimately, Maugham decided in favor of Gerald, and he and Syrie were divorced in 1929. Maugham experienced great tension over his sexual life, all the more so because it appears that he always felt much guilt over his homosexuality.

Maugham was of the generation for whom Oscar Wilde (1854–1900), the Irish-born playwright, poet, critic, and wit, exemplified what happens when one gives in to homosexual urges. Wilde's trial for sodomy—a result of his challenging the word of his lover's father, who had publicly denounced him—resulted in his ruin and ultimate death. Maugham never forgot what happened to Wilde. He also never forgot the severe strictures against homosexuality that persisted in England throughout his lifetime. For this reason, among others, he chose to live most of his life in the somewhat more tolerant atmosphere of France.

If Maugham's bisexuality was not known, would evidence of Philip's homosexual inclinations be found in the text of *Of Human Bondage*? It is impossible to answer this question now, with the facts of Maugham's life established beyond any doubt, but certainly even the details of Mildred's description, small as they are, might raise questions in the mind of the discerning reader. Philip's admiration for Griffiths, along with his tendencies toward masochism and voyeurism, are written large enough for no one to mistake. The biographical evidence merely supports what a careful reading of the novel suggests.

Another aspect of the relationship between Philip and Mildred also deserves mention—the marked difference in social class. Social class differences are as important in English fiction as in any other body of national literature. They play an especially important part in romantic attachments, with conflicts developing out of the differences between the wealth or social background of lovers. Marriage is completely unthinkable in some cases unless (by a convenient miracle) one party or the other in the relationship suddenly develops the proper credentials through an unexpected inheritance or a sudden realization that there is noble blood coursing through those common veins.

Philip is both attracted to and repelled by Mildred's commonness. From early in the novel, Philip is depicted as a creature of his class. Weeks makes fun of his middle-class version of Christianity—"In England dissenters aren't gentlemen, are they?" he asks Philip (113). In Heidelberg and in Paris alike, his values are constantly being challenged by a different moral reality. In his attraction to Mildred, he feels that he is giving in to a degree of baseness in his character to which her low social standing and vulgarity appeal.

Early in his relationship with Mildred, Philip thinks, "He had read of the idealization that takes place in love, but he saw her exactly as she was. She was not amusing or clever, her mind was common; she had a vulgar shrewdness which revolted him, she had no gentleness nor softness" (285). Philip goes on to think about her exaggerated table manners, her "passion for euphemisms," her affected politeness, all of which mark her as of a lower class. Later, having determined that he must have sexual relations with her, Philip thinks that perhaps he can have them only through marriage, and the thought of marriage to a waitress appalls him: "He had middle-class instincts, and it seemed a dreadful thing to him to marry a waitress. A common wife would prevent him from getting a decent practice" (301). Later still, in an argument over her affair with Griffiths, she accuses him of not being a gentleman, and he snaps, "What d'you suppose I care if I'm a gentleman or not? If I were a gentleman I shouldn't waste my time with a vulgar slut like you" (368).

From Mildred's standpoint, it is a point in Philip's favor that he is (most of the time) a gentleman. She is "impressed" that his father was a doctor and his uncle a vicar, but "at the same time was never quite comfortable in his presence; she could not let herself go, and she felt that he was criticizing her manners" (473). She has had her "fling," and now she is "quite ready to settle down with Philip. When all was said, he was a gentleman in every sense of the word, and that was something not to be sneezed at, wasn't it?" (474) Mildred is puzzled, however, by Philip's insistence that their relationship remain platonic and tries to explain his decision in different ways; in fact, that decision stems as much from their class difference and Philip's dread of marrying a waitress as from anything else.

Ultimately, it is on the issue of their continence that their relationship, such as it is, fails. Mildred is unable to understand Philip's reluctance to have sex with her, especially since earlier in their relationship he tried so hard to convince her that he wanted her. When he comes home slightly drunk one evening, she tries to seduce him but fails; afterwards, she "called him every foul name she could think of" in "language so obscene that Philip was astounded; she was always so anxious to be refined, so shocked by coarseness, that it had never occurred to him that she knew the words she used now" (479). She calls him first a "mug" (slang of the period for "chump" or "jerk") and then, in her final insulting utterance, "cripple." And there, except for several pathetic scenes, the tortured relationship between Philip Carey—now grown more independent, more free—and Mildred Rogers, in a fatal downward curve, ends.

In their final encounters—which the novel might do better without—Mildred is a full-fledged prostitute suffering from venereal disease. (Maugham euphemistically resists mentioning it by name.) Philip himself has gone through a difficult period of financial need, working in a department store to see himself through and interrupting his medical training. In these final pages, Mildred becomes the type of the fallen woman unredeemed in popular fiction, her fate clear and inescapable.

If the relationship between Philip and Mildred is at the core of the novel, it does not provide the final word on Philip's sexual character or on sexual love. If it did, the novel would end tragically, with Philip forever doomed to repeat the mistakes of the past and unable to form a truer, more lasting, relationship with anyone. Indeed, he does miss one opportunity for just such a relationship in the course of his affair with Mildred.

He meets Norah Nesbit, a writer, after his first disastrous episode with Mildred, and they soon become intimate friends. She is only slightly older than he, separated from her husband and earning her living by writing the Victorian equivalent of Harlequin romances. She is not pretty, in fact has rather odd features, but she is intelligent and witty, and Philip enjoys her company immensely. In contrast with Mildred, Norah is his intellectual equal. She is also more nearly of the same class, though somewhat down in her luck.

Philip and Norah become lovers—his first such relationship with a woman since his adolescent tryst with Emily Wilkinson—and yet remain friends. Norah has a "maternal instinct" (317) satisfied by her love for Philip. Philip, for his part, does not love Norah passionately but is "extremely fond of her" (318) and regards her as "the most charming friend he had ever had, with a sympathy that he had never found in a man" (319). To him, Maugham writes, the sexual relationship "completed" their friendship, "but was not essential."

Philip, of course, is still in bondage to Mildred, and ultimately that bondage ruins his relationship with Norah. Norah declares her love for him, but Philip, with Mildred once again in his life, this time pregnant, can only express his regrets that things have come to this pass. He admits he never loved Norah as much as she loved him, and then goes on to generalize: "There's always one who loves and one who lets himself be loved" (346). Though later, after Mildred's affair with Griffiths, he tries to revive the affair, by then it is too late. Norah has already met somebody else and plans to remarry.

The conflict Philip feels over his affair with Norah might be easier to interpret properly if one follows Ted Morgan's suggestion and views the story of Philip and Mildred as a disguised version of a homosexual romance. In that case, what Philip feels toward Norah is a strong sense of friendship in which their sexual relations are only one, not too essential part; toward the original of Mildred he feels a genuine passion that remains unfulfilled or unfulfillable. If Philip's dilemma is seen as that of a person who cannot decide between a woman and a young man, his decision to reject Norah makes more sense.

At any rate, the essential elements of his relationship with Norah—including an inequality of affection and a maternal spirit on the part of the woman—both enter into his final and most enduring affair, which does end in marriage, though the elements are mixed slightly differently. This time the woman is even more strongly maternal in spirit than is Norah, and the inequality is not so much of affection as of sexual role. Sally Athelny looks at the relationship between men and women in highly conventional terms, and in this she is influenced by the philosophy of her father, Thorpe Athelny.

Philip's relationship with Mildred is unequal in the sense that he loves her far more than she loves him; with Norah it is unequal in the sense that she loves him more than he loves her. With Sally, the degree of affection is more nearly equal, but the sexual roles are not. They follow conventions that are almost primitive. When he and Sally first have sex, in the midst of the hopfields of Kent on a warm summer evening, it is as if they return to ancient times: "The earth gave forth its freshness. There was something strange in the tremulous night, and something, you knew not what, seemed to be waiting: the silence was on a sudden pregnant with meaning. Philip had a queer feeling in his heart, it seemed very full, it seemed to melt . . . he felt happy and anxious and expectant" (594). The suggestion in this passage of a return to primitive times leads naturally to a view of Sally as a kind of earth mother: "He did not know what there was in the air that made his senses so strangely alert; it seemed to him that he was pure soul to enjoy the scents and the sounds and the savours of the earth. He had never felt such an exquisite capacity for beauty" (594). Sally's voice is "the voice of the country night itself." And later, at the time they come together again: "He was convinced of her purity. He had a vague inkling that many things had combined, things that she felt though she was unconscious of, the intoxication of the air and the hops and the night, the healthy instincts of the natural woman, a tenderness that overflowed, and an affection that had in it something maternal and something sisterly! and she gave all she had to give because her heart was full of charity" (598).

Eventually this mystic union must measure up to the standards of society. Eventually Philip and Sally must decide whether to marry or not. Sally turns out not to be pregnant, but Philip chooses marriage because he loves her, not because he feels an obligation to her. In their sexual union there has been a naturalness that Philip has not found with anyone else. The major question that their relationship raises for the reader is whether, perfect as it seems, it is believable.

Theodore Dreiser had fulsome praise for Maugham's achievement in *Of Human Bondage*, but doubts about Sally Athelny:

> Until the coming of Sally Athelny, all has been described with the utmost frankness. No situation, however crude or embarrassing [by the standards of the day], has been shirked. In the matter of the process by which he arrived at the intimacy which resulted in her becoming pregnant not a word is said. All at once, by a slight frown, which she subsequently explains, the truth is forced upon you that there has been a

series of intimacies which have not been accounted for. After Mildred Rogers and his relationship with Norah Nesbit, it strikes one as strange.[16]

Dreiser seems to have missed the significance of the metaphorical passages from the hopfields cited above, but perhaps what he is really saying is that the relationship with Sally is so idealized compared with the other relationships in the book that it seems scarcely to belong.

Philip has already decided that for him marriage is not a possibility. He will go off to sea and settle for a pattern different from the regular one that marriage and children and a home would provide. But in the end it is precisely that which the author provides for him. Is Maugham seeking a happy ending for the story to satisfy his readers? Each reader must decide if this is what he has done, but for many the novel would be more satisfactory, if less happy, if Philip and Sally did not marry.

Thematically, however, it is possible to justify the ending in one way. The greatest loss in Philip's life (as in Maugham's) occurs with the death of his mother. With Norah he regains some of that love, though on a different level, and with Sally, at last, he has found the eternal earth mother who will replace his first real mother, lost to him forever. On this level, perhaps the ending makes sense, but in terms of Philip's character as we have come to know it throughout the book, it is difficult to accept.

8

PHILIP'S PHILOSOPHY

In *The Summing Up* (1938), Maugham's first and best-written volume of memoirs, the author devotes a considerable number of chapters to the development of his philosophical thinking. He describes a practical philosophy, a means of dealing with everyday situations, not a vast metaphysical system of the type that would appeal to the professional philosopher. In detail as well as in general outline, Maugham's philosophy is remarkably similar to the one that Philip Carey evolves in *Of Human Bondage*. What is Philip's philosophy? How is it related to the experience of life depicted in the pages of the novel? By the end of the story, does Philip or the reader know the meaning of it all?

Like many young people, Philip begins life with certain unquestioned assumptions. He has had the disadvantage of being orphaned and having a disability, but he has lacked neither fundamental material comforts nor a decent enough education. He assumes that the world consists of essentially two classes of people: those with manners and good moral values and those without them. People in the first category are middle class or better and high church; they are also, almost invariably, English. The second, less-favored category includes the lower-middle class and below, who are likely to be dissenters or foreigners. At the time Philip begins his formal education, that is about the extent of his moral universe.

His first questions are about religion, and they begin in the most personal way with his observation that faith may be enough to move mountains but not to fix his foot (55) and then that his uncle's style of life is at variance with his principles (82). As a small boy, Philip learns that prayer is not powerful enough to change all things, no matter how sincere. As a somewhat older boy, about to try for a scholarship to Oxford, he is persuaded against the life of a vicar by the example of his uncle and other vicars he has observed.

More fundamental questions of religious belief occur after Philip reaches Heidelberg, in the course of his discussions with Hayward and Weeks. Hayward approaches religion as he approaches everything—as an aesthetic experience; it is not so much truth that he seeks as beauty, and beauty is to be found in ritual and in mystic revelation, not in rational commitment to a particular set of principles. At Cambridge, Hayward came under the influence of the ideas of John Henry (Cardinal) Newman (1801–90), the famous English convert to Roman Catholicism and author of many books, including the classic religious autobiography *Apologia pro Vita Sua* (1864), and toyed seriously with following in Newman's footsteps but was deterred by "fear of his father's wrath" (106). He still has sympathy with Roman Catholicism, however, and compares "favorably its gorgeous ceremonies with the simple services of the Church of England" (111). He believes, as he sums it up for Philip and for Weeks, in "the Whole, the Good, and the Beautiful" (112).

Weeks, by contrast, approaches religion as a fundamentally rational experience, in which one decides as systematically as possible upon a set of beliefs. As a Unitarian, he does not accept the idea of the trinity and is allied with an old tradition in American thought inclined toward skepticism rather than dogma. Weeks comes from Harvard, where the Divinity School, until the 1870s, was the chief seat of Unitarianism. He is also sympathetic toward the scientific approach to religion argued by the French historian and critic Ernest Renan (1823–92), whose *Vie de Jésus* (1863) he gives Philip to read (114).

Weeks likes to puncture holes in Hayward's unfounded assertions of belief, and Philip, in spite of his sympathy for Hayward, cannot help but see that, using the Socratic method, Weeks makes a stronger case. Once Philip comes to see that his religion is largely a matter of "environment and example" (117), his decision not to believe in God follows almost inevitably. The effect of the decision is to give Philip a sense of liberation; he has gone further than either Hayward or Weeks, he thinks, and it seems to him that "the whole world . . . was spread before him, and he was eager to step down and enjoy it. He was free from degrading fears and free from prejudice. He could go his way without the intolerable dread of hell-fire" (118). Every "action of his life" is no longer "a matter of urgent consequence. He could breathe more freely in a lighter air. He was responsible only to himself for the things he did" (118). With the irony of youth, he thanks God for no longer having to believe in him.

The realization that he no longer believes in God is Philip's major philosophical step during his year in Heidelberg, but the year also exposes him to many new ideas. He is introduced to the formal study of philosophy by attending lectures on Schopenhauer (1788–1860), author of *The World as Will and Idea*, by Kuno Fischer (1824–1907), a famous professor of philosophy. He attends the theater for the first time and sees, among others, the work of the influential and controversial Norwegian playwright Henrik Ibsen (1828–1906), then performed in Germany as much as anywhere else in the world, and that of Hermann Sudermann (1857–1928), a German playwright influenced by Ibsen. Through Hayward, he reads or hears about many of the works important to the aesthetes of the later nineteenth century. He does not, however, accept Hayward's ideal of the religion of art.

For many thinkers of the latter part of the nineteenth century, for whom conventional religious belief had become impossible, art provided a substitute. They saw in it the possibility of an aesthetic and moral order that science and materialism could not provide, and they saw in such figures as the German composer Richard Wagner (1813–83) new gods to worship. Wagner, much influenced by Schopenhauer, argued for a new form of opera that would be a *Gesamtkunstwerk*, or total work of art, embracing drama and music. (It is Wagner whose work Philip's tutor Professor Erlin finds so amusing [100]). The English

Pre-Raphaelite Brotherhood—which shaped in various ways the work of so many of the artists Hayward admires—was but one such group formed during the nineteenth century as a reflection of this kind of thinking; it was a secular religious order whose purpose was to celebrate not a god but a particular ideal of beauty.

Philip is exposed to the same principles in slightly different form in Paris in the person of Clutton, who seeks mystically for a new artistic form, the precise nature of which eludes him. "We paint from within outwards," he tells Philip. "If we force our vision on the world it calls us great painters; if we don't it ignores us; but *we* are the same. We don't attach any meaning to greatness or to smallness. What happens to our work afterwards is unimportant; we have got all we could out of it while we were doing it" (242). Philip imagines Clutton growing "bitter, lonely, savage, and unknown" in future years, still arguing his case for his own aesthetic views.

Philip in the end is too practical to take art as his religion—and also too practical to believe he can practice art when his talent is only mediocre. Of more importance to the development of his philosophy of life while he is in Paris is his exposure to the alcoholic poet Cronshaw. Cronshaw not only provides Philip (and the book) with a central metaphor for the meaning of life—the Persian carpet first referred to at the end of one of their most important discussions (213)—he also advances Philip's thinking several steps. In particular, he helps Philip to refine the distinction between society and the individual will.

In the same discussion that ends with the parable of the carpet, Cronshaw asks Philip what he thinks is the purpose of life, to which Philip replies: "I suppose to do one's duty, and make the best possible use of one's faculties, and avoid hurting other people" (208). Cronshaw points out that Philip has merely restated the Golden Rule. "It has nothing to do with Christianity," Philip asserts. "It's just abstract morality." No, Cronshaw insists, "You have thrown aside a creed, but you have preserved the ethic which was based upon it."

At this point Cronshaw moves on to a larger point about free will, the existence of which he denies: "The illusion which man has that his will is free is so deeply rooted that I am ready to accept it. I act as though

Philip's Philosophy

I were a free agent. But when an action is performed it is clear that all the forces of the universe from all eternity conspired to cause it, and nothing I could do could have prevented it. It was inevitable" (209). In fact, he goes on, what contains and shapes the will more than anything else is society: "Because we are gregarious we live in society, and society holds together by means of force, force of arms (that is the policeman) and force of public opinion (that is Mrs. Grundy [a character from an eighteenth-century play, representing conventional English morality]). You have society on one hand and the individual on the other: each is an organism striving for self-preservation. It is might against might" (210).

In such a world, all is reduced finally to self-interest: "You will find as you grow older that the first thing needful to make the world a tolerable place to live in is to recognize the inevitable selfishness of humanity" (210). Cronshaw carries the point even further: "Men seek but one thing in life—their pleasure" (211). Philip denies this point of view hotly, but Cronshaw insists. Even the self-denying act is not truly self-denying, he says; it is a form of deferred selfishness, a hope that by doing good for others one will do good for oneself.

If everyone is selfish, and the Golden Rule never applies, then what is the purpose of life? It is at this point in the discussion that the reference to the Persian carpet first occurs in the novel. "You were asking just now what was the meaning of life," Cronshaw says. "Go and look at those Persian carpets, and one of these days the answer will come to you" (213).

None of Cronshaw's ideas is particularly original, and yet to Philip they are influential. We must keep in mind that Philip is only twenty years old and that he still bases most of his judgments on highly conventional standards. It is not long until we can see the direct influence of Cronshaw's ideas in Philip's own thinking.

After Fanny Price's suicide, when Philip has begun to question whether he should stay in art school or not, he goes with his friend Flanagan to the Bal Bullier, a kind of dance hall, in Montparnasse. Flanagan's purpose is to cheer Philip up after what has happened; as Philip looks at the crowded floor and the sweating faces of the people, however, he thinks only that Cronshaw was right:

They danced furiously. They danced round the room, slowly, talking very little, with all their attention given to the dance. The room was hot, and their faces shone with sweat. It seemed to Philip that they had thrown off the guard which people wear on their expression, the homage to convention, and he saw them now as they really were. In that moment of abandon they were strangely animal: some were foxy and some were wolflike; and others had the long, foolish face of sheep. Their skins were sallow from the unhealthy life they led and the poor food they ate. Their features were blunted by mean interests, and their little eyes were shifty and cunning. There was nothing of nobility in their bearing, and you felt that for all of them life was a long succession of petty concerns and sordid thoughts. (238)

Cronshaw's comment on pleasure comes back forcibly to Philip's mind: "The desire for pleasure . . . urged them blindly on, and the very vehemence of the desire seemed to rob it of all pleasure" (239). This bestial spectacle seems to justify all that Cronshaw has said.

Back at Blackstable, after the death of his aunt and just before his entrance to medical school, Philip has much time to himself—time to read and to think, time to attempt to absorb the experiences of the past two years in France. During this period, he reads primarily philosophy, following no particular plan. He reads Thomas Hobbes (1588–1679), the English philosopher best known for his *Leviathan* (1650), delighting in his "robust common sense" (258); Benedict Spinoza (1632–77), the Dutch philosopher (whose essay "On Human Bondage" provides the title of the novel), who in Philip's view has a mind "noble, . . . unapproachable and austere" (258); and David Hume (1711–76), Scottish philosopher, whose skeptical philosophy, founded in the rationalism of the Enlightenment, appeals to Philip much as a novel would.[17] On a different level, he absorbs the philosophical history of George Henry Lewes (1817–78), an important editor of the Victorian period and author of *Life of Goethe* (1855), who asserted the importance of the connection between the life of a philosopher and his thought: "When you knew that [the man he was], you could guess to a great extent the philosophy he wrote" (258). Philip also reads *The Origin of Species* (1859) by Charles Darwin (1809–82), whose scientific theories proposed the idea of evolution. With

Darwin's work, Philip is "intensely moved by the grandeur of the struggle for life, and the ethical rule which it suggested . . ." (259).

As a result of this period of reading and thought, Philip decides that truth is relative; the important thing is to know yourself: "It looked as though you did not act in a certain way because you thought in a certain way, but rather that you thought in a certain way because you were made in a certain way. Truth had nothing to do with it. There was no such thing as truth. Each man was his own philosopher . . ." (258). It also leads him to a maxim that Maugham had once devised for himself: "Follow your inclinations with due regard to the policeman around the corner" (257).

Following Cronshaw's ideas discussed earlier, Philip feels (especially after reading Darwin) that might is right: "Society stood on one side, an organism with its own laws of growth and self-preservation, while the individual stood on the other. The actions which were to the advantage of society it termed virtuous and those which were not it called vicious. Good and evil meant nothing more than that" (259).

Society has three major weapons against the individual: "laws, public opinion, and conscience" (259). The first two of these can be met by the individual with "guile," but "conscience was the traitor within the gates" (259). The state and the individual are irreconcilable opposites: "*That* [Maugham's italics] uses the individual for its own ends, trampling upon him if he thwarts it, rewarding him with medals, pensions, honours, when he serves it faithfully; *this*, strong only in his independence, threads his way through the state, for convenience's sake, paying in money or service for certain benefits, but with no sense of obligation; and, indifferent to the rewards, asks only to be left alone" (259). The conclusion is obvious: "if for the individual there was no right and no wrong, then it seemed to Philip that conscience lost its power. It was with a cry of triumph that he seized the knave and flung him from his breast" (260).

What do Philip's ruminations about the individual and the state have to do with his experience as depicted in the novel? They occur just as he is about to begin his study of medicine. He is now twenty-one, in his majority, and about to begin his affair with Mildred Rogers. Norah

Nesbit and Sally Athelny are still ahead, the affair with Emily Wilkinson well behind.

In school, at Tercanbury, he certainly felt the weight of an organized hierarchical system on himself, and found, as all school boys find, how difficult it is to achieve individual rights under such circumstances. His year of apprenticeship in accountancy may also have contributed to his thinking about the power of an established system over the individual, but that year came to an end and Philip had a relatively easy out. His time without money in the department store is far ahead, and his years in Paris are relatively free from pressures of this kind.

With all this in mind, one wonders why he makes so much of the individual versus society. What relevance does this idea have to the Philip the reader knows by chapter LIII? The answer to that question lies in another passage in the same chapter, Maugham's personal experiences, and the probable year when Philip begins medical school.

In the second paragraph of chapter LIII, Philip reflects on his uncle's accusation that he is guilty of flippancy. Of course he is flippant, having become so as a way of dealing with pain—the pain of "great loss he had sustained in the death of his father and mother," the pain of life among strangers in which "he had seldom been used with patience or forbearance," the pain of "mockery of his fellows" at school (256). He has been lonely because of the "disillusion and the disappointment caused by the difference between what it [the world] promised to his active imagination and what it gave."

One of the chief causes of "disillusion and disappointment" in Maugham's life, along with the death of his mother and the unhappiness of his upbringing, was his bisexuality. At the time he was writing *Of Human Bondage* Maugham was about to begin his lifelong affair with Gerald Haxton; when, like Philip, he was about to begin medical school he had already experienced his first homosexual affair with Ellingham Brooks. And in 1895, when he was in his third year of medical school, the arrest and trial of Oscar Wilde—an event that impressed Maugham for the rest of his life—took place. Maugham was twenty-one at the time, the precise age of Philip in chapter LIII.[18]

Maugham seems to have transferred to Philip his own emotions at the time of the Wilde trial. By 1895, he knew his own sexual nature and was attempting to deal with it. Then came the spectacle of the great Wilde dragged down by his own unwillingness to compromise, to let a nasty accusation pass. In Wilde's case, the policeman was no longer around the corner; society, its will thwarted, was ready to trample on him. In one's conscience there may be no right or wrong, but it makes little difference to the individual who is still unable to follow his own inclinations. Maugham says that for all his thoughts on freedom and the individual will Philip is no closer to knowing the meaning of life. Does he mean that Philip is no closer to resolving his personal dilemma?

Perhaps Philip's thoughts in chapter LIII seem unrelated to his experience because his full experience is not revealed to the reader. There is an obvious disproportion between what Philip has done (or even what he is about to do) and what he is thinking at this point in the novel. If, however, his thoughts are read in the context of Maugham's own sexual experience and his reaction to the trial of Wilde, they make much more sense.

For all his assertion of free will, Philip does not, in dealing with Mildred, behave like someone who is free. Freedom (to the extent that Philip is to know it) does not come for him until considerably later in the book, when by chance he meets Thorpe Athelny. From that point onward, however, his entire viewpoint changes under the influence of this unusual and eccentric man.

Athelny does not argue an "abstract morality"; what he stands for is a set of values, a way of life, which is difficult to sum up intellectually. In some ways it is a profoundly antiintellectual set of values; yet intellectual experience does have a part in it. It has some features of the theory of the life force, a post-Darwinian concept popularized by writers such as George Bernard Shaw (1856–1950), the equivalent in social terms of the theory of natural selection. However, Athelny's set of values is perhaps best summed up by the phrase "domestic hedonism."

The hedonist believes that the chief purpose of life is the pursuit of pleasure. (This is Cronshaw's argument.) For Athelny, pleasure takes the form of a domestic arrangement in which he is the centerpiece and everything is focused on the satisfaction of his needs. To a certain extent, this arrangement is typical of the period of which Maugham is writing; what makes Athelny's unusual is the extreme to which he carries it and the extent to which he makes it the cornerstone of a philosophy of life.

Athelny has a large family and follows the "antique" custom of dining by himself. His wife (by common law) is not a lady, but the daughter of a farmer who has "never bothered about aitches in her life" (428). She has born twelve children of whom nine are living, and Athelny imagines she will bear even more. Her sole purpose in life is to bear children and cook food and keep house. Athelny's views might even raise the ire of Phyllis Schlafly: "You want a wife who's an intellectual equal," he says to Philip. "Your head is crammed full of ideas of comradeship. Stuff and nonsense, my boy! A man doesn't want to talk politics to his wife, and what do you think I care for Betty's views upon the Differential Calculus? A man wants a wife who can cook his dinner and look after his children" (428–29).

Athelny strikes an analogy from nature with the legend of the halcyon: "When the kingfisher, flying over the sea, is exhausted, his mate places herself beneath him and bears him along upon her stronger wings. That is what a man wants in a wife, the halcyon." The woman is allowed greater strength, but she remains completely unequal to the man.

Next to his primitive domestic arrangement, Athelny's greatest enthusiasm is for Spain. The furnishings of his household are in the Spanish style, and he looks on Spanish culture as his ideal. He is especially enthusiastic about the painting of El Greco (ca. 1541–1614), and Philip is struck by a reproduction of the painter's famous view of the city of Toledo: "He felt strangely that he was on the threshold of some new discovery in life. He was tremulous with a sense of adventure. He thought for an instant of the life that had consumed him: love seemed very trivial beside the excitement which now leaped in his heart" (435).

Here, in the Spain that Athelny conjures up for him, is a new sort of idealism: ". . . something better than the realism which he had adored; but certainly it was not the bloodless idealism which stepped aside from life in weakness; it was too strong; it was virile; it accepted life in all its vivacity, ugliness and beauty, squalor and heroism; it was realism still; but it was realism carried to some higher pitch, in which facts were transformed by the more vivid light in which they were seen"

(437). Philip, having been hurt twice by Mildred, sees that the human will can still exist: "He seemed to see that a man need not leave his life to chance, but that his will was powerful; he seemed to see that self-control might be as passionate and as active as the surrender to passion; he seemed to see that the inward life might be as manifold, as varied, as rich with experience, as the life of one who conquered realms and explored unknown lands" (437).

To Philip, Athelny's life has the virtue of "perfect naturalness" (438); it certainly reflects an extremely conservative view of marriage or of any other relationship between men and women. As the tension between Maugham's selves increased, so did a negative attitude toward women in his work. In his next novel, *The Moon and Sixpence* (1919), that attitude becomes outright misogyny; in *Of Human Bondage*, it is reflected both in Thorpe Athelny's views and in the actual relationship between Philip and Sally. The notion of "perfect naturalness" implies a highly traditional relationship, in which the roles are precisely defined. Philip's and Sally's roles do not appear to be precisely the same as Thorpe's and Betty's, but they have many of the same qualities, at least in incipient form.

Before their relationship is formed, however, and after Philip's fortunes reach their lowest ebb, he reviews once again his choices in life and comes to what amounts to his final conclusion on the matter. Now he thinks he understands at last what Cronshaw meant by the Persian rug: "As the weaver elaborated his pattern for no end but the pleasure of his aesthetic sense, so might a man live his life, or if one was forced to believe that his actions were outside his choosing, so might a man look at his life, that it made a pattern" (524). Life in fact has no meaning. One chooses for the sake of choosing, not because one choice is better or necessarily more important than another:

> Out of the manifold events of his life, his deeds, his feelings, his thoughts, he might make a design, regular, elaborate, complicated, or beautiful; and though it might be no more than an illusion that he had the power of selection, though it might be no more than a fantastic legerdemain in which appearances were interwoven with moonbeams,

that did not matter: it seemed, and so to him it was. In the vast warp of life . . . with the background to his fancies that there was no meaning and that nothing was important, a man might get a personal satisfaction in selecting the various strands that worked out the pattern. (524)

Philip sees two fundamental alternatives: "There was one pattern, the most obvious, perfect, and beautiful, in which a man was born, grew to manhood, married, produced children, toiled for his bread, and died; but there were others, intricate and wonderful, in which happiness did not enter and in which success was not attempted; and in them might be discovered a more troubling grace" (524–25). Is Maugham alluding here to the same thing he seems to suggest elsewhere? Hayward's is the first example of a life lived with a "more troubling grace," and Cronshaw's follows. In the end, happiness does not matter any more than pain: "They came in, both of them, as all the other details of his life came in, to the elaboration of the design" (525).

The reader fully expects Philip to follow the less traveled path, but then his love for Sally changes all of that, with a last-minute turnaround that is not entirely convincing: "He thought of his desire to make a design, intricate and beautiful, out of the myriad, meaningless facts of life: had he not seen also that the simplest pattern, that in which a man was born, worked, married, had children, and died, was likewise the most perfect? It might be that to surrender to happiness was to accept defeat, but it was a defeat better than many victories" (607).

Years later, in *The Summing Up*, Maugham answered the same question in approximately the same way:

If anyone should ask me what is the use or sense of this pattern I should have to answer, none. It is merely something I have imposed on the senselessness of life because I am a novelist. For my own satisfaction, for my amusement and to gratify what feels to me like an organic need, I have shaped my life in accordance with a certain design, with a beginning, a middle and an end, as from people I have met here and there I have constructed a play, a novel or a short story. We are the product of our natures and our environment. I have not made the pattern I thought best, or even the pattern I should have liked to make, but merely that which seemed feasible.[19]

Whether Philip has chosen the more feasible alternative or developed a truly consistent philosophy is something that every reader of *Of Human Bondage* must decide. He has at least found something of meaning to his life; perhaps, to follow his interpretation of the riddle posed by Cronshaw, we can ask for nothing more.

9

MATTERS OF *STYLE*

A writer should always begin with what he knows about. Out of my experience as a medical student in a London slum's hospital, I wrote *Liza of Lambeth,* which came out when I was 23. For most young writers, the most valuable material they have is in their recollections of childhood. You never see any characters for the rest of your life as clearly as you see the ones you associated with when you were a child.[20]

Maugham made these remarks in an interview in 1949; they point to a truth about his conception of the novel and, specifically, about the novel closest to his own childhood experiences. *Of Human Bondage,* as the story of the development of a young man who is at least at one point a would-be artist, conforms to the characteristics of the bildungsroman; it also conforms strikingly to the prevailing tendency in the history of English fiction—that of realism.

Volumes have been written in definition of the term *realism.* This is not the place to pursue such a theoretical question, but it may be useful to pause a moment to consider some of the implications of the term. The novel as a literary form is intended, at least in part, to tell us what is new.

(The Latin root of *novel* is *novus,* meaning "new.") To give us news, the novel must come close to the lives of its readers—they must be able to identify in some way with what happens to the characters—and to public events of the day. Even when novels move in the direction of fantasy or romance, they must be grounded in details that make the most outlandish plot seem credible.

Dickens, Eliot, Thackeray, Trollope, and the other great English novelists of the nineteenth century wrote for a middle-class audience and, especially in the case of Dickens, frequently used the novel to move that audience toward social change. Dickens exposed social ills in his novels—mistreatment of children and the poor, the vagaries and lassitude of the government and the courts—but he also engaged the reader in the lives of his characters. The work of Dickens and the other great Victorians thus represents at the same time a social history of the Victorian period and extremely satisfying reading.

Maugham's conception of the novel in *Of Human Bondage* shares some of these characteristics, though it is primarily realistic in its portrayal of Philip Carey's personal dilemma and only secondarily concerned with history and the dynamics of social change. In representing Philip's problems and their resolution, however, it draws on some of the stock devices of Victorian fiction, especially with the inherited money and marriage that both come at the end of the novel.

Of Human Bondage also reflects to some extent the standards of another major body of fiction, French naturalistic fiction of the nineteenth century. Naturalism is realism carried one step further, frequently with an emphasis on the most unpleasant aspects of life. It is also heavily deterministic—which is to say that, unlike much Victorian fiction, it suggests that the individual will makes no difference.

The medical school chapters of *Of Human Bondage* in particular present a picture of life in all its hopelessness. Philip sees the potentiality of the people he works with but also sees their despair. They are "like clay in his hands" (399), and, generally, they have little choice about what happens to them. Philip thinks the death of one patient is inevitable "because the man was a little wheel in the great machine of a complex civilization, and had as little power of changing the circumstances as an automaton" (401).

The same quality of inevitability is emphasized toward the end of the book when Philip, having made a bad investment of his little remaining money, is forced into working in a department store and living the life of the clerks who work there. It is at this point in the novel, his thoughts gloomy and his only hope the fact that his uncle may soon die, that Philip decides life has no meaning; it is at this point in the novel, faced by the endless line of customers and wearied by the monotony and mindlessness of his work, that Philip himself nearly reaches a state of total despair.

Dickens and the Victorian realists suggested in their work that a change in social conditions would mean a change in the life of the poor; Maugham—influenced in this respect by the naturalists—sees chiefly the hopelessness of their state. They will never change, nor will the conditions that lead them to this state. Change in *Of Human Bondage* comes for the exceptional individual, to some extent as a result of chance; it is not something brought about by legislation or moral outrage.

If thematically Maugham's novel is not precisely Victorian in outlook, in technique, as in certain features of its plot, it reflects some of the most common Victorian practices. For a novel published in 1915, it is in fact old-fashioned. It is clear that Maugham was primarily interested not in the form of what he was writing but in its content. Nothing illustrates this more clearly than what he does with point of view.

All novels—in fact, all works of fiction, whatever their form—are written from a particular point of view. It may be first person or third (or even occasionally second); it may be in the voice of a character or in the voice of the author; it may reflect multiple points of view—whatever the case, the author must make a decision fairly early in the writing of a work of fiction about how to tell the tale. By 1915, it was common enough to follow the pattern of Flaubert in *Madame Bovary* (1857). He wrote what is essentially a third-person narrative almost entirely from the viewpoint of one character, the frustrated woman of the title, who, unhappy in her marriage to a country doctor, has a series of increasingly destructive love affairs.

The advantage of this technique, later refined by such novelists as Henry James (1843–1916) and James Joyce (especially in his *A Portrait of the Artist as a Young Man*), is the concentration it affords. The reader sees, smells, touches, thinks through the consciousness of a single character. Love him or hate him, by the end of *A Portrait of the Artist,* you know Stephen Dedalus, Joyce's central character, through and through. At no point in the novel does Joyce shift from the viewpoint of Stephen, not even during a scene in which a priest delivers a long sermon on the horrors of hell; even there, the priest's words are quoted just as Stephen would hear them.

Maugham, on the other hand, takes Victorian liberties with point of view, shifting from Philip to other characters when he wishes—even sometimes within the same chapter—and (also very much in the Victorian manner) writing from the viewpoint of the author himself. In his foreword to *Of Human Bondage,* he says that one reason he gave up writing for the theater to write the book was "the wide liberty of the novel" (6). It gave him the space he needed for a very personal book; in his freedom with point of view, perhaps he expresses another aspect of that yearning for freedom that is so much a feature of Philip Carey.

Maugham's freedom with viewpoint asserts itself quite early in the novel—in chapter V, for instance, after the young Philip has moved to Blackstable to live with his uncle and aunt. This chapter, though very short, reflects at least three different points of view: Philip's, with which it begins; his uncle's, to which it shifts after the first few sentences; and, finally, his late mother's, in the anecdote about the photographs that closes the chapter. In chapter VIII, where Philip rebels for the first time against the tyranny of his uncle in the matter of the blocks, the viewpoint teeters between Philip and his uncle in the early pages of the chapter, only to shift abruptly after the line "I hate you. I wish you was dead" (33) to his aunt.

The novel abounds in examples of this kind of shift. Sometimes, the shift is obviously for dramatic effect, not simply narrative convenience, as, for instance, when Maugham writes from Mildred's viewpoint in chapter XCVI, when she and Philip have the argument that terminates with her calling him a cripple. By entering into her character at this moment in the story, Maugham increases the effect of the final scene in the chapter, which is really the climax of their relationship.

Given the degree of liberty Maugham takes, one can argue that the prevailing point of view in the novel is that of the author—not just when he is obviously intruding on the narrative to make the kind of comment only an author can make, but at all times. In chapter XCVI, for example, Mildred is thinking of the fact that Philip has not wanted sexual relations with her: "Then came the conversation," Maugham writes, "in which he told her that he intended their relations to be platonic . . ." (474). This is not Mildred thinking in Mildred's words; this is Maugham telling us what Mildred thinks at that particular time. Or, later in the same chapter, when she thinks further on the same topic: "Mildred was not a woman who conceived the possibility of compassion, generosity, or kindness. Her only conclusion was that Philip was queer" (475). Here Maugham is forming a judgment of Mildred, passing it on the reader in his own words. These are but two examples of a phenomenon that occurs repeatedly throughout the novel, often much more obviously.[21] In many of his later novels, Maugham wrote from the viewpoint of the author as teller of tales; it gave him an omniscience that he needed to move a story along. In *Of Human Bondage*, the authorial presence may not always be so obvious, but the viewpoint is omniscient in the same way as in the later work.

Occasionally the author's voice intrudes so forcibly into the narrative that it becomes totally separate, almost distinguishable by quotation marks. This sort of intrusiveness is especially characteristic of the Victorian novel and is often called the "dear reader" syndrome. In chapter XXV, for instance, Philip is thinking of Monsieur Ducroz, one of his tutors in Heidelberg, and the author comments: "He was so young, he did not realize how much less is the sense of obligation in those who receive favours than in those who grant them" (102–3). This sort of aphoristic comment is possible only on the part of the author (or narrator, in first-person stories). It occurs again in chapter XXXII, in reference to Philip's inexperience in dealing with women and Emily Wilkinson's consequent advantage over him: "A greater experience than Philip's would have guessed from these words the probabilities of the encounter: the distinguished writer invited to luncheon *en famille,* the governess coming in sedately with the two tall girls she was teaching" (134).

Much later, at the beginning of chapter XCVIII, the passage could be written by Dickens himself (though it lacks his stylistic touch): "And now it happened that the fortunes of Philip Carey, of no consequence to any but himself, were affected by the events through which his country was passing" (484). These are especially obvious instances of the viewpoint that may be said to prevail throughout the whole novel: the author's voice that in the end dominates.[22]

In style and tone, Maugham is straightforward, even somewhat predictable, in a manner consistent with his chronological, realistically detailed narrative. Sentences tend to follow the subject-verb-object pattern, though they are frequently compound or complex in structure. Inversion and other structural variations occur chiefly in the form of occasional questions in the text; there is no attempt at highly complex structure. (Maugham does create some long sentences by stringing a series of clauses together with semicolons, but the clauses themselves are seldom very complex.) There is also little tendency toward exotic vocabulary. In his foreword to the novel, Maugham says that with *Of Human Bondage* he began to write prose different from that of his earlier novels—prose of "plainness and simplicity" rather than prose "jewelled" and of "a rich texture": "With so much that I wanted to say within reasonable limits I felt that I could not afford to waste words and I set out now with the notion of using only such as were necessary to make my meaning clear" (6).

Maugham's intention notwithstanding, there are many passages in the text of *Of Human Bondage* in which the meaning is not clear and the prose labored or filled with tautologies. A passage quoted previously may suffice to illustrate: "The thing then was to discover what one was and one's system of philosophy would devise itself. It seemed to Philip that there were three things to find out: man's relation to the world he lives in, man's relation with the men among whom he lives, and finally man's relation to himself. He made an elaborate plan of study" (258). In this passage, intended to define for the reader Philip's philosophical musings just before medical school, the second sentence is especially awkward and unclear. What is the distinction between the first phrase after the colon ("man's relation to the world he lives in") and the second ("man's relation with the men among whom he lives")? What the author intends (one can guess from the context) is a distinction between the phenomenal world, or world of the senses, and the social world, or world of other people, but the language of the passage does not make this distinction clear. Furthermore, the wording of the second phrase is extremely clumsy; Maugham could just as easily have said "man's relation to other men" and let it go at that.

Other examples of clumsiness and tautology occur in the same short passage. The word "thing" is followed shortly by "things"; "thing" is a vague word in most contexts, and in its first occurrence in Maugham's text it is redundant. Nothing is said in the first sentence of the paragraph until the infinitive "to discover." The shift in the passage from "one" to "man" is also awkward, though obviously intended to make the three points following the colon more general in their application.

Perhaps it is unfair to single out a short passage from a novel of such length and use it as the basis of a general criticism, but this is a crux passage (in a crux chapter) and it is unfortunately all too typical of the stylistic flaws to be found in the novel as a whole. These lapses tempt one to the observation that it was no wonder Dreiser reviewed the book with such favor; he was also noted for the awkwardness of his style.

Generally, however, a more important characteristic of the style of *Of Human Bondage* is that it disappears: the reader becomes so absorbed in the story Maugham has to tell that he does not especially notice the style of the telling. And Maugham's claim in his foreword that his theatrical experience led him to seek a greater succinctness of style is clearly justified by the many scenes in the novel that show the dramatist's touch.

Victorian novels often begin with long passages of exposition introducing the reader to the main characters or to the setting of the story. Maugham shows his dramatist's flair at catching attention by opening his long novel very abruptly with a short description of the day, followed immediately by the beginning of the action. The reader follows the half-awake Philip to his mother's bedside, experiencing the sad day of her death with him. At no point in the early pages of the novel is there any extended passage of exposition. What exposition there is—providing background on Philip's parents' lives or his uncle's feelings about them—is tucked into scenes occurring ostensibly in the present time of the narrative. The gain in immediacy is obvious; the reader is involved at once in Philip's story by the events of his mother's death, his move to Blackstable, his new life there. The novelist, his technique shaped in part by his experience of writing for the stage, is following the frequently repeated dictum: "Show, don't tell."

Throughout the novel, the same principle holds at key moments in the story. In particular, much of the relationship of Philip and Mildred is developed not through exposition but through dialogue, as in a play. Through such scenes the reader gains a better sense of both characters. Maugham also frequently uses a line of dialogue to cap a scene, to bring it to a resounding conclusion. Mildred's "Cripple!" (480), at the end of the chapter in which they have their important final difference, is a good example of this technique.

The vividness of the dialogue in the novel helps to offset the occasional monotony of the prose style and the general sameness of tone. Now and then a certain archness enters into the tone of the writing, as, for instance, in the description of Hayward's past life early in the novel:

> Then Hayward went to London to read for the bar. He had charming rooms in Clement's Inn, with panelled walls. . . . He had ambitions that were vaguely political, he described himself as a Whig, and he was put up for a club which was of Liberal but gentlemanly flavor. His idea was to practice at the Bar (he chose the Chancery side as less brutal), and get a seat for some pleasant constituency as soon as the various promises made to him were carried out; meanwhile he went a great deal to the opera, and made acquaintance with a small number of charming people who admired the things that he admired. (107)

In this passage words like "charming," "vaguely," "gentlemanly," and "pleasant" convey the sense of Hayward as effete and ineffectual. Similar sarcasm creeps into descriptions of Uncle William.

Another quality that enters into the tone, especially in scenes involving Philip and Sally toward the end of the novel, is a sort of poetic lyricism that stands out in marked contrast with the tone of most of the rest of the book: "They turned a corner, and a breath of warm wind beat for a moment against their faces. The earth gave forth its freshness. There was something strange in the tremulous night, and something, you knew not what, seemed to be waiting; the silence was on a sudden pregnant with meaning" (593). On the whole, however, the tone of the writing is prosaic and completely in keeping with Maugham's stated intention of plainness and simplicity.

In the same sense, *Of Human Bondage* is a novel not particularly rich in poetic imagery or allusion. The use of poetic imagery in prose narrative was characteristic of most of Maugham's early novels and generally characteristic of prose fiction of the 1890s and the turn of the century. Maugham deliberately avoided such rhetorical strategies in writing the story of Philip Carey, and as a result the text has few instances of simile, metaphor, or other devices typical of poetic prose.

Maugham does develop patterns of language, however, that have a certain repetitive effect. One of these occurs in the use of the language of bondage to describe Philip's sensations at school and later in his affair with Mildred. This language, with its emphasis on pain, is an essential component of Philip's emotional life, and Maugham uses it in various contexts (my italics) to convey how Philip feels: "He was not crying for the *pain* they had caused him, nor for the *humiliation* he had suffered when they looked at his foot, but with rage at himself because, unable to stand the *torture,* he had put out his foot of his own accord" (45–46); "Singer was so much stronger that Philip was *helpless,* and he was always *forced* after more or less *torture* to *beg* his pardon" (48); "Though he dreaded *humiliation* more than anything in the world, he hugged himself for two or three days at the thought of the *agonizing* joy of *humiliating* himself to the Glory of God" (51); "He had thought of love as a rapture which seized one . . . but this was not happiness; it was a hunger of the soul, it was a *painful* yearning, it was a *bitter anguish,* he had never known before" (278); "if he [Philip] tempted them [Mildred and Griffiths] would yield, and he took a fierce joy at the thought of their dishonour. Though every word he spoke *tortured* him, he found in the *torture* a horrible delight" (375). These and many other instances of such language in the text form a repetitive pattern not unlike the refrain of a poem. They certainly constitute the most consistent and compelling pattern of language within the novel.

Another pattern of language relates to Cronshaw's Persian carpet. Again the references to the carpet are too literal to be called poetic, but they recur in various contexts to define Philip's developing philosophical position. Most striking, perhaps, is the passage in chapter CVI in which Philip thinks that he may choose the way of "a more troubling grace," beginning, "Whatever happened to him now would be more motive to add to the complexity of the pattern, and when the end approached he would rejoice in its completion" (525).

Sparse in poetic devices, the text of *Of Human Bondage* is also sparse in allusion. Some prose, like Joyce's, seem so rich in allusion to other texts that to read it is sometimes to read several authors at once. Maugham's text in this novel, on the other hand, is what it is: whatever allusion occurs, occurs chiefly to define character, not to enrich the text, and typically refers to familiar authors or texts.

Hayward, of all the characters, is most defined by allusion, because he is the character who is most "literary." Literary allusions abound in the sections devoted to him—especially to figures, like Pater, important to Hayward's vision of the aesthetic life. For instance, Maugham assumes the reader will recognize, in Hayward's letter to Philip just before he leaves for Paris, the reference to Pater's famous phrase from *The Renaissance:* "one should burn with the hard, gem-like flame" (168). Maugham also assumes, at the end of chapter XXVII, that the reader will recognize the significance of Weeks's giving Philip a copy of Renan's *La Vie de Jésus*. Significant as these references and allusions may be, they are an exception to the rule in the generally straightforward, unallusive text of *Of Human Bondage*.[23]

In many respects, Maugham's longest and most autobiographical novel has little in common with his other major novels. It was his first important statement in the form, and neither in content nor in length was it to be repeated. The other novels by Maugham still considered important enough to be read—*The Moon and Sixpence* (1919), *Cakes and Ale* (1930), and perhaps also *The Razor's Edge* (1944)—are much more concise and are narrated in the first person by a persona of the author. (In the last of them Maugham uses his own name.) Maugham distances himself greatly from his material, leaving the reader in no doubt that he is telling the tale, controlling the elements of the story from start to finish. While the author has the controlling voice in *Of Human Bondage*, his primary purpose is to get beneath the skin of Philip Carey; in the other novels, one sometimes feels that the author or his surrogate is there to keep the reader from the characters rather than lead the reader in.

10

THE SUMMING UP

"No author has more cleverly converted his defects into assets. . . ."[24] Angus Wilson made that remark in a preface to a collection of short stories by Maugham, but, as a general truth, it could stand as a judgment of Maugham's entire body of work, including *Of Human Bondage*. No assessment of the ultimate worth of this novel, Maugham's major achievement in the form (and probably his major achievement, period), can avoid recognizing its flaws. The final question must be whether the novel's flaws outweigh its artistic assets.

A good deal of one's feeling about *Of Human Bondage* depends upon one's reaction to Philip. Is it possible to remain sympathetic to a character who allows himself to be used—even abused—by a woman who clearly doesn't love him? Can the compassion of the reader survive Philip's tendency toward self-punishment, bringing so much unpleasantness on himself? The most important character in *Of Human Bondage*, around whom the entire story is built, at times seems weak and will-less and never shows anything but the slightest glimmer of a sense of humor. How many books of such length are so unleavened by flashes of wit?

At the same time, however, Philip ultimately has the courage to change, to recognize that his behavior is self-destructive, and to do something about it. Furthermore, much of Philip's behavior toward Mildred—like his behavior toward his patients—is the result of a desire to help another human being in distress or dire straits. While his desire to take on the responsibilities of fathering Mildred's child has a perverse, voyeuristic side, it also reflects a genuine impulse to care for someone, to take over when no one else is willing to do so. In Christian terms—which Philip never completely escapes—he is anxious to perform charitable acts, even to the point that they become self-damaging. Out of similar impulses many have been sainted. Can we criticize Philip for wanting to do good?

And the good, with a curious, ironic twist that we don't necessarily expect in the bleak universe that Maugham sketches in the philosophical chapters of the novel, comes back to Philip just as it does in the Golden Rule: when he is down in his luck he is helped by the Athelnys, who want nothing more than to share whatever they have with him. Behind this gesture, and behind the new fortunes of Philip by the end of the novel, it is easy to imagine the often cynical Maugham smiling as he thinks that the universe, so capable of evil, is also, with equal neutrality of impulse, capable of good.

Some fiction writers, like some dramatists and composers, are known almost entirely for one work. They may have created a considerable body of work by the time they die, but all that survives in memory is one major achievement that for some reason overshadows everything else they have done. Maugham, though more than just a fiction writer, may be in this category. Although all his work is still in print, the evidence is that Maugham is remembered today primarily for one work and one work alone, his most personal achievement, however flawed—*Of Human Bondage*.

APPENDIX 1:
OF HUMAN BONDAGE:
THE MOVIE

The news is out: don't read the novel when it's assigned, don't even bother to read the *Notes*—get the movie in video. Made in 1934 by Radio Pictures, *Of Human Bondage* stars Bette Davis (in her first real starring role) as Mildred, Leslie Howard (probably best known for his role as Ashley Wilkes in the film version of *Gone with the Wind*) as Philip, and Frances Dee as Sally Athelny, with Reginald Owen as Thorpe Athelny, Reginald Denny as Harry Griffiths, Alan Hale as Emil Miller, and Kay Johnson as Norah Nesbitt. John Cromwell directed, and Leslie Cohen wrote the screenplay.

The eighty-three minute film provides far less than would even a cursory reading of the novel. To say that Maugham's story has been truncated for the sake of keeping down the length of the film is to put it mildly. To say that what is left is then freely interpreted is to put it accurately. The result bears some resemblance to the original, but pity the poor student who, required to read the book in school, decides to rely on the film version to take its place.

First of all, the scenario begins on about page 246 of the Penguin edition of the novel, as Philip, having studied art in Paris for several years, has almost reached the conclusion that he should abandon it. He asks Monsieur Foinet's advice, and Monsieur Foinet agrees to give it right then. This is the point—with a night-time café scene at variance with the time and place that Maugham describes in the novel—where the movie begins. Missing as a result are a whole series of important characters—including Uncle William and Aunt Louisa, Perkins and the other masters and students at King's School, Etheridge Hayward and the American

Weeks, Emily Wilkinson, Fanny Price, Cronshaw and other friends of Philip's in Paris—and a number of crucial events without knowledge of which Philip's subsequent behavior is difficult to interpret. These include first and foremost the death of his mother, his adoption by an uncle and aunt who are childless, his mistreatment by other students at school, and his first experiences of love.

The movie version concentrates on the relationship of Philip and Mildred, to the exclusion of practically everything else. This is the most memorable relationship in the book—ask anyone who has not read it in years what it's about and the answer will usually be something like, "Is that the one about the medical student who has the affair with the waitress?"—but to focus so exclusively on it is to show nothing but Philip's weakest side. Here, his only apparent reason for eventually leaving Mildred is not that he has some inner resolve to end their painful relationship but that he has met somebody else he loves more, Sally Athelny. Much of the time, in fact, Leslie Howard portrays Philip as if he were in a coma. Philip's lack of resolve is turned into a form of paralysis, and Howard stares at the camera as if he were drugged.

Virtually the only life in the film comes from Bette Davis's performance, and it is remarkable—given that this was her first real leading role (her previous films were unmemorable)—that her acting style was so well developed. The performance is almost pure Bette Davis, but is it Mildred?

Physically, Davis has little or no resemblance to the Mildred Maugham has described. She is neither boyish nor flat-chested, and (though the film is not in color) her hair looks more blond than red. Davis plays her part as a tart with a cockney accent that comes and goes. Mildred may grow to look like a tart as the novel progresses, but it is her false gentility—her genteelness—that Maugham emphasizes early on—the way she tries to look like a lady when she isn't one. Because Davis is more successful not looking like a lady at all, Mildred's personality is subtly distorted in her performance. There are some excellent moments, however, most notably in the final argument when Mildred lets go and reveals the real person beneath the facade. There, Davis's Mildred is totally believable, and Howard's Philip reacts accordingly.

Appendix 1: Of Human Bondage: The Movie

The other characters are a mixture of good and bad interpretations, sometimes not helped much by the inadequacies of the script. Kay Johnson is an appropriately motherly Norah, but Frances Dee as Sally seems too much the ingenue she was at the time the film was made. Sally should not look quite so well groomed. Reginald Owen as Thorpe Athelny is the best of the minor characters, partly because he has the most to work with. He has some vitality at least, and he looks the part he is playing, though the Athelnys' house is just a little too neat, their meal service just a little too fine.

The least successful of the minor characters is Reginald Denny as Harry Griffiths. To begin with, he is too old for Harry; there is nothing boyishly handsome about him. He comes on more like a traveling salesman than the languidly sensuous young man of Maugham's novel, who is successful with the ladies because he doesn't try too hard. Maugham's Harry tells amusing anecdotes to make the ladies relax. As Denny portrays him, you expect Harry to clap them on the back and tell dirty stories. But then the script accents Harry's seductiveness toward Mildred in such a way that broad touches are called for, and Denny obligingly provides them.

Some scenes in the movie are relatively faithful to the novel, even retaining some of Maugham's lines. The final argument between Mildred and Philip is a case in point. Others depart from his text, or are pure inventions for the sake of moving the story along or emphasizing some aspect of the theme that the audience might be presumed to miss otherwise. Just after the final argument, for instance, Mildred is seen destroying all of Philip's belongings. In the text, only the results of the destruction are described. Furthermore, in the film Mildred finds bonds that Philip's uncle had left him and burns them in the fireplace. In the novel there is no such detail.

In the novel Philip's foot is better after his operation, but he still limps slightly; in the film the operation seems to cure his problem completely. In the book it is clear that Mildred has venereal disease; in the movie—made when the production code was strict—the illness is changed to tuberculosis. A scene is added in the film, mainly to give Harry a chance to redeem himself, in which Harry helps to bring the dying Mildred to the hospital and then later tells Philip there is no use in his seeing her because she is already dead. Finally, there is no mention in the film that Sally thinks she is pregnant, no hint that Philip and Sally have had anything more than wholesome chats by the fireside.

There are some minor differences as well—a scene with Miller and Philip that is not in the book; pictures of nude women over Philip's fireplace rather than the picture of a nude man (Miguel Ajuria) that is the only thing Philip has saved from art school—but by now it should be clear that what the movie of *Of Human Bondage* gives the viewer is a bare outline of what the novel gives. The student who wants to look at the movie to save time might be better advised to read the novel but skip every other line.

APPENDIX 2:
CHRONOLOGY:
PHILIP CAREY'S LIFE

The chronology of events in Philip's life does not correspond precisely to that of Maugham's, but this is scarcely surprising, since Maugham created a fictional life for Philip and, no matter how autobiographical his account may be, there are bound to be differences between them. For one thing, fiction requires a shaping of events that life seldom provides. For another, no matter how autobiographical his work, an author will always suppress or edit certain details.

In *Of Human Bondage*, however, there are some special complications. In the first place, anachronisms occur because Maugham sometimes forgets that he is not following the chronology of events from his own life. Second, he sometimes seems to forget how he has dated an event, causing another form of error. Finally, in at least one major instance, he violates history, describing events that took place some time earlier as if they were contemporaneous with Philip's experience. For these reasons, a chronological table is more than pedantically useful.

The first anachronism in the text occurs at the beginning of chapter XIII, where Maugham put Philip's age at "nearly twelve" when he is in the first form of prep school. Maugham is probably thinking of his own birthdate, January 25, as Philip's, because he also refers to a time "after Christmas" when Philip will become the head boy. Two chapters later, however, Philip enters senior school at the age of thirteen. If his birthdate is to be construed as the same as Maugham's (an implication supported by the opening chapters of the novel), there is clearly a mistake, because he would be entering senior school one year later than he should, in 1889 instead of 1888.

Another anachronism occurs in chapter LIV of the Penguin edition, as Philip is entering medical school. Maugham writes, "When Philip went to St. Luke's *changes had recently been made* [my italics] in the regulations, and the course took five years instead of four as it had done for those who registered before the autumn of 1892" (263). Maugham is apparently thinking of his own entrance year to medical school, not Philip's, because, as the table at the end of this appendix shows, the year has to be 1896. By that date, changes that began in the autumn of 1892 would not be described as recent.

The precise age at which Philip enters medical school is a more complicated question. Toward the end of the book, as Philip passes his last examination and receives his diploma, Maugham writes, "It was seven years since he had entered St. Luke's Hospital. He was nearly thirty" (574). Maugham is counting the two years that Philip spent in the department store, as we learn just a few pages later when Philip says, in a conversation with Doctor South, "I didn't go in for the Medical till I was nearly twenty-three, and I had to give it up for two years in the middle" (576).

However, this contradicts the facts presented earlier in the novel, toward the end of the Paris chapters, when Philip first decides to enter medical school. In chapter XLVII, Philip is twenty-one (218). The month is March, as we learn from the first sentence in that chapter. Toward the end of the summer of the same year, Philip's aunt dies and he is called back to Blackstable, presumably in August, because his uncle refers later to the possibility that he will go back to Paris in September (253). (This in itself seems to contradict an earlier passage, after the summer interlude in Fontainebleau, when two months are supposed to have passed [246].) In chapter LIV, Philip arranges to enter St. Luke's "before the end of the summer session" (260). Thus, Philip is not nearly twenty-three when he enters medical school but just twenty-one; his age at the end of the novel must then be twenty-eight, not just short of thirty. (Maugham himself was well over thirty when he finished his own medical training.)

Another error, though a minor one, occurs in chapter CXII, when Philip, back in Blackstable for the funeral of his uncle, thinks of his mother "dead now for nearly twenty years" (555). In fact, since the date is now probably 1901, she has been dead only slightly more than fifteen years. (In this case, there is no contradiction with Maugham's life; his mother died in 1882 and his uncle in 1897, a difference of almost precisely fifteen years.)

The historical anachronism occurs in reference to events in the Paris art world, and particularly to the ascendancy of the impressionists. Philip is in Paris from 1894 to 1896, but the artistic and intellectual climate of which Maugham writes suits better the Paris of the late 1880s or very early 1890s. What Maugham describes might therefore confuse some readers knowledgeable of art history into thinking that the events in Philip's life occur earlier than they do.

Why are there so many errors of this kind in Maugham's text? And why, considering how long the novel has been in print, have they never been corrected? Maugham had to know that the art world he was describing in the novel was in fact of an earlier period; he knew art well—especially the art of the impressionists—and in real life was about to begin collecting it. As to the other errors, they seem of the kind that an author, in writing such a long work, might overlook in his first draft or even, if not pointed out to him, in subsequent revisions. It still seems strange, even under these circumstances, that there are so many.

On the occasion of his presenting the manuscript of *Of Human Bondage* to the Library of Congress in 1946, Maugham said, "I corrected the proofs in the autumn of 1914 . . . in a billet near Ypres by the light of a single candle, and since then I have opened the book once."[25] Perhaps we must take him at his word. In his foreword to the novel, Maugham says that he wrote it in the first place to rid himself of "teeming memories of my past life" (6). Writing it was an act of exorcism, and perhaps Maugham simply couldn't bear to look at it afterwards for details of chronology.

As to failures of editorship, we can only speculate. Why does the *New Yorker* magazine publish a special section about "our forgetful authors"? Because sometimes editors are forgetful, too.

The following table assumes that Philip is ten years old when he starts school at King's and twenty-one when he starts medical school at

St. Luke's. It establishes as accurately as possible under the circumstances the chronology of events in the novel and Philip's age at each stage.

YEAR (PHILIP'S AGE)	EVENTS (CHAPTERS IN NOVEL)
1885 (January) (10)	Mother dies (II)
1885 (September) (10)	Enters King's School, Tercanbury (X)
1887 (December) (12)	Enters first form (XIII)
1888 (13)	Enters senior school (XV)
1889 (14)	Encounter with Rev. Gordon (XVI)
1891 (16)	Confirmation class (XVII)
1892 (17)	Leaves for Heidelberg (XXII)
1893 (18)	Returns from Heidelberg and takes up accounting; affair with Emily Wilkinson (XXXII)
1894 (19)	Leaves for Paris (XL)
1896 (21)	Begins medical school and meets Mildred (LIV)
1899 (24)	Probable beginning date of hiatus in medical studies (XCVIII)
1901 (26)	Resumes studies (CXII)
1903 (29)	Completes medical school (CXVI)

NOTES

1. For the material in this chapter, I wish to express a general indebtedness to Maurice Beebe, *Ivory Towers and Sacred Founts: The Artist as Hero in Fiction from Goethe to Joyce* (New York: New York University Press, 1964) and François Jost, "The 'Bildungsroman' in Germany, England, and France," in *Introduction to Comparative Literature* (Indianapolis: Bobbs-Merrill, 1974), 134–50. Robert Lorin Calder looks at the same subject in his chapter, "*Of Human Bondage* and the Novels of Apprenticeship," in *W. Somerset Maugham and the Quest for Freedom* (Garden City: Doubleday, 1973), 78–130.

2. *W. Somerset Maugham: The Critical Heritage*, ed. Anthony Curtis and John Whitehead (London: Routledge and Kegan Paul, 1987), is a useful compendium of reviews and other critical comment. Also see *W. Somerset Maugham: An Annotated Bibliography of Writings about Him*, comp. and ed. Charles Sanders (De Kalb: Northern Illinois University Press, 1970).

3. Theodore Dreiser's "As a Realist Sees It" appears in abbreviated form in Curtis and Whitehead, 130–34. The complete review appears in *The Maugham Enigma*, ed. Klaus W. Jonas (New York: Citadel Press, 1954), 114–20.

4. Edmund Wilson, "The Apotheosis of Somerset Maugham," in *Classics and Commercials: A Literary Chronicle of the Forties* (New York: Farrar, Straus, 1958), 319. Strachey is quoted in Curtis and Whitehead, 1.

5. Wilson, 326.

6. *105 Greatest Living Authors Present: The World's Best*, ed. Whit Burnett (New York: Dial, 1950). The survey is discussed and summarized in "A Foreword in the Form of a Report," xi–xxv.

7. *Maugham*. (New York: Simon and Schuster, 1980). I wish to express a general indebtedness to Ted Morgan for the biographical data included in this study.

8. For a fuller discussion of the chronology of the novel and some of its difficulties, see Appendix 2.

9. D. H. Lawrence, *Sons and Lovers*, (New York: Viking, 1968), 36.

10. W. Somerset Maugham, *Cakes and Ale: Or the Skeleton in the Cupboard* (Garden City, N.Y.: Doubleday, 1930), 150.

11. George Orwell, *A Collection of Essays* (Garden City, N.Y.: Doubleday, 1954), 43.

12. For background on the French impressionists, see John Rewald, *The History of Impressionism*, 4th ed., rev. (New York: Museum of Modern Art, 1973).

13. William H. Masters, Virginia E. Johnson, and Robert C. Kolodny, *Human Sexuality*, 2d ed. (Boston: Little, Brown, 1985), 645.

14. Masters, Johnson, Kolodny, 650.

15. Morgan, 196.

16. Curtis and Whitehead, 133.

17. On Spinoza's influence on the thought of Cronshaw, see Calder, 118–21.

18. Morgan, 36–38.

19. W. Somerset Maugham, *The Summing-Up* (Garden City, N.Y.: Doubleday, 1938), 293.

20. Harry Gilroy, "How to Write—By Maugham," in Jonas, 47.

21. There are many examples. Look closely, e.g., at the passage on the painfulness of puberty quoted at length in chapter 5 of this text.

22. Cf., e.g., Anthony Trollope, *The Last Chronicle of Barset*, ed. Stephen Gill (Oxford: Oxford University Press, 1984), the beginning of chapter XV:

> Some kind and attentive reader may perhaps remember that Miss Grace Crawley, in a letter written by her to her friend Miss Lily Dale, said a word or two of a certain John. "If it can only be as John wishes it!" And the same reader, if there be one so kind and attentive, may also remember that Miss Lily Dale had declared, in reply, that "about that other subject she would rather say nothing"—and then she had added, "When one thinks of going beyond friendship,—even if one tries to do so,—there are so many barriers!" From which words the kind and attentive reader, if such reader be in such matters intelligent as well as kind and attentive, may have learned a great deal with reference to Miss Lily Dale. (140)

23. The precise source of Maugham's biblical quotation (52) is unknown; it reads like the King James version, but is not.

24. In Angus Wilson's introduction to *Cakes and Ale and Twelve Short Stories* (Garden City, N.Y.: Doubleday, 1967), 7.

25. Jonas, 126.

BIBLIOGRAPHY

Primary Sources

Of Human Bondage was originally published simultaneously in New York and London in 1915. It is currently available in a number of editions, but the most generally available is the Penguin edition used for this study. (See my comments under Notes on References and Acknowledgments.) I list immediately below other works by Maugham, many of which are referred to in my text, in their first editions. Most of these works are available to the reader in modern editions or reprints. The film version of *Of Human Bondage* is available on videotape from Goodtimes Home Video Corporation.

Novels

Liza of Lambeth. London: T. Fisher Unwin, 1897.

The Making of a Saint. Boston: L. C. Page, 1898.

The Hero. London: Hutchinson and Co., 1901.

Mrs. Craddock. London: William Heinemann, 1902.

The Merry-go-round. London: William Heinemann, 1904.

The Bishop's Apron. London: Chapman and Hall, 1906.

The Explorer. London: William Heinemann, 1907.

The Magician. London: William Heinemann, 1908.

Of Human Bondage. New York: George H. Doran, 1915.

The Moon and Sixpence. London: William Heinemann, 1919.

The Painted Veil. New York: George H. Doran, 1925.

Cakes and Ale. London: William Heinemann Ltd., 1930.

The Narrow Corner. London: William Heinemann Ltd., 1932.

Theatre. Garden City, N.Y.: Doubleday, Doran and Company, 1937.

Christmas Holiday. London: William Heinemann Ltd., 1939.

Up at the Villa. New York: Doubleday, Doran and Company, 1941.

The Hour Before the Dawn. Garden City, N.Y.: Doubleday, Doran and Company, 1942.

The Razor's Edge. Garden City, N.Y.: Doubleday, Doran and Company, 1944.

Then and Now. London: William Heinemann Ltd., 1946.

Catalina. London: William Heinemann Ltd., 1948.

Short Fiction

Orientations. London: T. Fisher Unwin, 1899.

The Trembling of a Leaf. New York: George H. Doran, 1921.

The Casuarina Tree. London: William Heinemann Ltd., 1926.

Ashenden: Or The British Agent. London: William Heinemann Ltd., 1928.

Six Stories Written in the First Person Singular. Garden City, N.Y.: Doubleday, Doran and Company, 1931.

Ah King. London: William Heinemann Ltd., 1933.

Cosmopolitans. Garden City, N.Y.: Doubleday, Doran and Company, 1936.

The Mixture as Before. London: William Heinemann Ltd., 1940.

Creatures of Circumstance. London: William Heinemann Ltd., 1947.

The Complete Short Stories of W. Somerset Maugham. 3 vols. London: William Heinemann Ltd., 1951.

The Complete Short Stories of W. Somerset Maugham. 2 vols. Garden City, N.Y.: Doubleday and Company, 1952.

Nonfiction

The Land of the Blessed Virgin. London: William Heinemann, 1905.

On a Chinese Screen. New York: George H. Doran, 1922.

The Gentleman in the Parlour. London: William Heinemann Ltd., 1930.

Don Fernando. London: William Heinemann Ltd., 1935.

The Summing Up. London: William Heinemann Ltd., 1938.

Strictly Personal. Garden City, N.Y.: Doubleday, Doran and Company, 1941.

A Writer's Notebook. London: William Heinemann Ltd., 1949.

The Writer's Point of View. London: Published for the National Book League by the Cambridge University Press, 1951.

The Vagrant Mood. London: William Heinemann Ltd., 1952.

Bibliography

Ten Novels and Their Authors. London: William Heinemann Ltd., 1954. [American title *The Art of Fiction*.]

Points of View. London: William Heinemann Ltd., 1958.

Purely for My Pleasure. London: William Heinemann Ltd., 1962.

Selected Prefaces and Introductions of W. Somerset Maugham. Garden City, N.Y.: Doubleday and Company, 1963.

Plays

A Man of Honour (written 1898; revised 1902; produced 1903).

Lady Frederick (1903; produced 1907).

Mrs. Dot (1904; 1908).

Jack Straw (1905; 1908).

Penelope (1908; 1909).

Smith (1909).

The Tenth Man (1909; 1910).

Grace (1910).

The Land of Promise (1913).

Our Betters (1915; 1917).

Caroline (The Unattainable) (1915; 1916).

Love in a Cottage (1917; 1918).

Caesar's Wife (1918; 1919).

Too Many Husbands [British title *Home and Beauty*] (1919).

The Circle (1919; 1921).

The Unknown (1920).

East of Suez (1922).

The Camel's Back (1923).

The Constant Wife (1926).

The Letter (1926; 1927).

The Sacred Flame (1928).

The Breadwinner (1930).

For Services Rendered (1932).

Sheppey (1933).

The Collected Plays of W. Somerset Maugham. 3 vols. London: William Heinemann Ltd., 1952.

Posthumous Works

Maugham, W. Somerset. *A Traveller in Romance: Uncollected Writings, 1901–1964.* Ed. John Whitehead. New York: Clarkson N. Potter, 1984.

Seventeen Lost Stories by W. Somerset Maugham. Compiled and with introduction by Craig V. Showalter. Garden City, N.Y.: Doubleday and Company, 1969.

Secondary Sources

Beebe, Maurice. *Ivory Towers and Sacred Founts: The Artist as Hero in Fiction from Goethe to Joyce.* New York: New York University Press, 1964. A critical survey of the apprenticeship novel as applied to the artist.

Brander, Laurence. *Somerset Maugham: A Guide.* New York: Barnes and Noble, 1963; reprint 1965. An overview of the author's achievement first published shortly before his death.

Brophy, John. *Somerset Maugham.* (Writers and their Work series.) Rev. ed. London: London: Longmans, Green, 1958. A provocative, though brief (pamphlet-length), essay on Maugham's achievement.

Brown, Ivor. *W. Somerset Maugham.* London: International Textbook Co., 1970.

Burnett, Whit, ed. *105 Greatest Living Authors Present: The World's Best.* New York: Dial Press, 1950.

Burt, Forrest D. *W. Somerset Maugham.* English Authors Series. Boston: Twayne, 1985.

Calder, Robert Lorin. *W. Somerset Maugham and the Quest for Freedom.* Garden City, N.Y.: Doubleday, 1973. An exceptionally thorough survey of Maugham's work emphasizing the theme of freedom.

Cordell, Richard A. *Somerset Maugham: A Writer for All Seasons.* Rev. ed. Bloomington: Indiana University Press, 1969. A heavily biographical study of Maugham's achievement now in most respects superceded by Ted Morgan's biography.

Curtis, Anthony. *The Pattern of Maugham: A Critical Portrait.* New York: Taplinger, 1974. Another biographical study of Maugham's achievement; like Cordell's, less an assessment than an appreciation.

———. *Somerset Maugham.* New York: Macmillan, 1977. A coffee-table book survey of Maugham's life and works with many photos.

———. *Somerset Maugham.* Writers and Their Work series. Windsor, Berkshire, England: Profile Books, 1982. A pamphlet-length treatment of Maugham's work, apparently to supercede Brophy's work above.

Bibliography

Curtis, Anthony, and John Whitehead, eds. *W. Somerset Maugham: The Critical Heritage*. London: Routledge and Kegan Paul, 1987. An anthology of critical reviews of Maugham's work.

Jonas, Klaus, ed. *The Maugham Enigma: An Anthology*. London: P. Owen, 1954. A collection of interviews and critical pieces.

————, ed. *The World of Somerset Maugham*. Westport, Conn.: Greenwood Press, 1959. Another anthology of critical pieces.

Jost, François. *Introduction to Comparative Literature*. Indianapolis: Bobbs-Merrill, 1974.

Masters, William H., Virginia E. Johnson, and Robert C. Kolodny. *Human Sexuality*. 2d ed. Boston: Little, Brown, 1985.

Morgan, Ted. *Maugham*. New York: Simon and Schuster, 1980. The definitive biography.

Naik, M. K. *W. Somerset Maugham*. Norman: University of Oklahoma Press, 1966. A biocritical study arguing that cynicism spoils much of Maugham's work.

Rewald, John. *The History of Impressionism*. 4th ed., rev. New York: Museum of Modern Art, 1973.

Sanders, Charles, ed. *W. Somerset Maugham: An Annotated Bibliography of Writings about Him*. De Kalb: Northern Illinois University Press, 1970.

Stott, Raymond Toole. *A Bibliography of the Works of W. Somerset Maugham*. Rev. ed. London: Kaye and Ward, 1973.

Wilson, Edmund. *Classics and Commercials: A Literary Chronicle of the Forties*. New York: Farrar, Straus, 1958.

INDEX

This is an index to biographical, literary, and historical allusions, chiefly names and titles, in my text. I have excluded references to themes, characters, and places in *Of Human Bondage* because I feel these would be repetitious and redundant in a book devoted to an extended discussion of all three. I have also excluded all references to any of the above items when they occur in a quoted passage. In addition, I have limited references to the "Notes" section to important names not already cited in the body of the text.

My single exception to these rules is the inclusion of the term *bildungsroman*. The concept it embodies is so central to my reading of *Of Human Bondage* that I feel it must be part of this index.

Index

Greco, El (Domenico
Theotocopoulos), 37, 72

Hale, Alan, 89
Haxton, Gerald, 19, 56, 70
Heep, Uriah, 35
Hilton, James: *Goodbye, Mr. Chips,*
26
Hobbes, Thomas: *Leviathan,* 68
Howard, Leslie, 89–90
Hughes, Thomas: *Tom Brown's
School Days,* 26
Hume, David, 68
Huxley, Aldous, 11

Ibsen, Henrik, 65
Ingres, Jean-Auguste: *Odalisque,*
38

James, Henry, 79
Johnson, Kay, 89, 91
Johnson, Virginia E., 50–51
Jost, François, 97n1
Joyce, James, 2–3, 85; *A Portrait of
the Artist as a Young Man,*
2–3, 23, 79

Kant, Emmanuel, 6
Kelly, Gerald, 37

Lawrence, D. H., 3; *Sons and Lov-
ers,* 2, 23
Lewes, George Henry: *Life of
Goethe,* 68

Mackenzie, Compton, 3; *Sinister
Street,* 2, 10
Manet, Edouard: *Olympia,* 38
Masters, William H., 50–51
MAUGHAM, W. Somerset
Cakes and Ale, 24, 85
Cosmopolitans, 37
Don Fernando, 37
Liza of Lambeth, 8, 41
The Moon and Sixpence, 37,
73, 85

The Razor's Edge, 85
The Summing Up, 63, 74
Meredith, George: *The Ordeal of
Richard Feverel,* 2, 34
Morel, Paul, 23
Morgan, Ted, 55, 60; *Maugham,*
18–20
Mürger, Henri: *La Vie De Bohème,* 36

Newman, John Henry (Cardinal):
Apologia pro Vita Sua, 64
New Republic, 10

Orwell, George: "Such, Such Were
the Joys. . . ," 26–27
Owen, Reginald, 89, 91

Pater, Walter, 36; *Marius the Epicu-
rean,* 34; *The Renaissance,* 85
Pontifex, Ernest, 2
Pre-Raphaelite Brotherhood, 9, 38–
39, 65–66
Puccini, Giacomo: *La Bohème,* 36

Renan, Ernest: *La Vie de Jesus,* 64, 85
Rewald, John, 98n12
Rossetti, Dante Gabriel, 38–39
Ruskin, John, 34

Schopenhauer, Arthur, 6; *The World
as Will and Idea,* 65
Shaw, George Bernard, 11, 71
Spinoza, Baruch (Benedict), 6; "On
Human Bondage," 68
Strachey, Lytton, 11
Sudermann, Hermann, 65

Thackery, William Makepeace, 77;
The History of Pendennis, 2
Trollope, Anthony, 77

Wagner, Richard, 65
Wales, Prince of (later Edward VII), 43
Wilde, Oscar, 57, 70–71
Wilson, Angus, 87
Wilson, Edmund, 11–12

ABOUT THE AUTHOR

Archie K. Loss is professor of English at The Pennsylvania State University in Erie, The Behrend College. He is the author of books on Joyce (*Joyce's Visible Art*, 1984) and Maugham (*W. Somerset Maugham*, 1987), as well as numerous articles and reviews in the field of modern literature.